WHAT I'VE LEARNED FROM NEVER HAVING A Boyfriend

STACEY SPRINGOB

Happy Reading!
#LUB
Stacey Springob

Printed by CreateSpace, an Amazon.com Company
Charleston, South Carolina
Printed in the United States of America
www.createspace.com
Cover Design: Stacey Springob and Amanda Springob

ISBN-13: 978-1496175557
ISBN-10: 1496175557

TABLE OF CONTENTS

TABLE OF CONTENTS CONTINUED

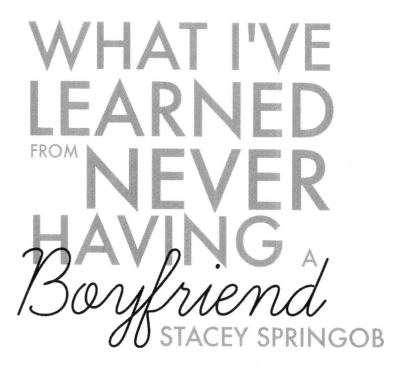

WHAT I'VE LEARNED

FROM **NEVER HAVING** A *Boyfriend*

STACEY SPRINGOB

Thank you:

MOM, DAD, AND AMANDA

MY FRIENDS AND FAMILY

FAYTHE AND KATRINA

MY HOMETOWN

THE DON'T CHA KNOWS

THE REAL DORMWIVES OF WILLY P

YOUTUBE, TED TALKS,
THE HOLLYWOOD REPORTER ROUNDTABLES,
AMANDA DE CADENET, BETHENNY FRANKEL,
LADY GAGA, AND BEYONCÉ

AND ANY PERSON WHO BOUGHT A BOOK,
FOLLOWED ME ON SOCIAL MEDIA, OR SHARED
MY MESSAGE WITH SOMEONE

"YOU OWN EVERYTHING THAT HAPPENED TO YOU. TELL YOUR STORIES. IF PEOPLE WANTED YOU TO WRITE WARMLY ABOUT THEM, THEY SHOULD'VE BEHAVED BETTER."

-Anne Lamott

ROMANTICIZING

My sister Amanda once told me that I'm a 'romanticizer.' I tend to take an instance out of life and change it into a magical or more colorful moment with my thoughts and ideas. I "make something a bigger deal when it's really just black and white." I have to "make it all lovey-dovey and magical when it's just the facts."

Amanda's right. I'm a romanticizer. But you know what? I like that about myself. Sometimes, I think it's `good to be a romanticizer, because I think it keeps things in check with what's really important to us in life. It has reminded me to find the good in life when it is not going as planned...such as when I'd thought I'd be in a relationship by now, but I'm not.

I have decided after being thirteen and awkward, sixteen and socially lost, and nineteen trying to find my niche that love affects everything. We sing songs about it, pin quotes on Pinterest about it, and text each other until midnight about it. I have decided after graduating high school and going through college that everyone has a relationship status, however relationship statuses are no longer just labeled as you're single or you're taken. Some people have been in an on-again-off-again relationship for two years, some people are in long distance relationships and only see each other twice a year, some people have a special person they talk to every single day but are not boyfriend/girlfriend with, and some people are single and in love with their best friend.

This is why I like being a romanticizer, because it's my way of being a storyteller. I get to take time to discuss those thoughts we have as we are walking to class, when we're on our lunch break, or driving in our car for hours. I believe the gaps between our thoughts about college, work, friend drama, family life, money, and everything else is why we as the youth of today understand each other. Because while we all have different goals and motives, the things we think about in between the principal parts of life are all the same.

If someone would've told me ten years ago that before I turned the age of twenty-one, I'd write a book, live in both Los Angeles and New York City, see Beyoncé and Lady Gaga in concert, attend the American Music Awards, high-five Jimmy Fallon on *The Tonight Show*, get an internship offer from CNN, or report live on the news station I grew up watching, I probably would have believed you; I did everything prior to those moments to make that story believable. If someone would've told me ten years ago that I'd still be single today, my story would have made me feel defeated.

During the in-between moments of my story, I've

realized that as much as I have been successful, I am also very much an in-betweener.

Even though I've found a lot of success, all I really have ever wanted at the end of the day is love. In high school I never felt like that cool girl who could get the jock, and in college I'm definitely not the sorority girl posing next to the sexy frat boy on Instagram. But I'm also not a nerdy person who found a Sheldon Cooper love story. I'm just in the middle, and that's not a place I'm ever at in any other life category.

But then I was at lunch one day in the middle of my freshman year of college, when my friend started complaining about her boyfriend. And she said something to me that changed my life. As I was indulging in my spinach salad, Rachel said, "You have it made because since you're single you only have to worry about yourself, but I *always* have to make sure that everything I do will be okay with my boyfriend."

And then I walked back to my dorm thinking I could write a book about all the things I've learned from *not* having a boyfriend. And I became completely okay with being a part of that middle category with love; in fact, I started embracing it.

This book is for that girl who has always been in a relationship since she was thirteen years old. This book is for the guy who sleeps around. This book is for those people who are a lot like me; the in-betweeners, the ones still trying to figure out what a love life really is.

I thought sharing my story and my experiences of being single for this long would be useful to other people.

We often only get the viewpoints of those who have been committed to someone before, but we don't always get to see it from an outside source who has never had the experience. My wish for this book is not to hurt people's feelings if I mention experiences in their lives or how they affected my life, but for people to understand that when one has never had a person to call their own, I notice the good, the bad, and the ugly in other people's relationships and love lives. However, I won't count myself out on this one; I plan to share stories about my love life (if you can even call it that) as well. If this book can help one person straighten out their love life, then I will never regret sharing what I've observed from other people in my life over the years. As a writer I see ordinary events as contributions to the ideas I want to share, and these people and their experiences are the contributions to my story.

I believe I am the same but different. I have things to say about relationships because I've seen a lot while never having experienced it myself. I see my love life at an angle many others don't see their own, and I believe it can be of value for other people to hear about. I want to share my stories of what I've seen, in order to help others learn more about themselves or avoid making the same mistakes. I am a nice person, I work extremely hard, and like I said before, I'm someone you'd expect to be just as busy dating as I am going after my goals. But I'm not. So here's my story.

I just feel that love is something we all talk about. We have sleepovers and created cookie dough ice cream for nightlong conversations about love. We write songs about love, and we save every text message about love so we can refer back to it. It's what we fall asleep thinking about and wake up hoping to feel by someone sleeping next to us. Even though I'm still single, I'm often the person giving people advice about their boyfriends, girlfriends, breakups, or even other people's single lives. I've seen a lot and felt a lot in my own years of aloneness, and I think my singular viewpoint is something worthy for people to hear. I'm not single because I'm a crazy psycho. I'm single for some reason I'm still trying to figure out. So think of me as your Dumbledore, your Mr. Feeny, your Oprah, or your Morgan Freeman as I share with you what I've learned from never having a boyfriend.

Oh and for the record, I'm not a lesbian. Sorry ladies.

EVERYTHING IS YOUR STORY

It took three guys, a lot of nerds, too many crazy people, and several old married couples to teach me about love.

Carson, Sean, and Brad…those are the three males I let into my life, my brain and my heart, then out of my life, then back into my life again; but always in my heart and my brain. They completely emulate the types of guys I think every girl meets at some point in her life; there was the perfect (and I mean perfect) guy, the guy who's your best friend, and the douche bag.

Brad was the douche bag. He's the guy who tripped me when I thought I could tell the idiots from the good ones. I met him freshman year of college in speech class. From the moment I heard him say that he loved the Packers and hated Obama, I knew he would be a character. Somehow I managed to get his attention by the end of my first college semester, and we went out for dinner. Everything went great although I think we talked about everything you're not supposed to talk about on a first date, from past relationships to politics. But then the texting and talking dwindled away, and I wondered if I did something wrong in that he no longer liked me. So I asked, and he said he wasn't interested in dating anyone at that time.

As I started moving on from that minor letdown in my life, about a month later Brad messaged me again. So of course we started up talking regularly. We'd hang out several times then we'd fizzle out. And this cycle repeated itself multiple times over the course of about two years. It included lots of overanalyzing on my end, me driving across the state of Wisconsin a couple times to see him, too many drunk texts at 3 A.M. from Brad to count, and really just a lot of bullshit; and yet, moments that I still miss from time to time.

After two years of these shenanigans, we fully called things quits. This time though, it was for good; no friendship afterwards, nothing. I deleted Brad's number; I unfollowed him on social media. I wanted this guy officially out of my life. But I am a girl, and we ladies like to Facebook stalk; and I'm really good at it (so good if the FBI ever needs a professional Facebook stalker, I'm their girl). So I admittedly Facebook creeped on Brad once in a while, hoping to only find him posting crap about the same stupid shit I never cared about and *not* about any new lady in his life. But then one day karma bit me in the ass when I ran my cursor over his name on Facebook and it said "in a relationship". I may have had a minor panic attack, realizing this loser who had no issue coming in and out of my life for two years was now willing to commit to someone…someone who wasn't me.

Sean was this big shouldered, sexy rugby player. He was my first kiss and one of the nicest guys I've ever met. We went to the same high school and always had this unspoken attraction to each other, but it never went anywhere. But then we saw each other at a graduation party when he was a freshman in college and I a junior still in high school. We exchanged numbers, and soon we were texting everyday. Sean was that guy I could tell anything to and he wouldn't judge. We ended up going to the same university and hung out a lot. He was my getaway from my psycho roommate, and he made me realize that love isn't about how perfect someone is, it's about being able to wear sweatpants and no makeup in front of someone who won't care. Sean taught me the idea of companionship in a relationship versus just finding Prince Charming. I wanted to date him, but he often avoided the subject. So we remained good friends. While I was studying abroad my sophomore year of college, he was dating a girl named Morgan. Morgan was a bitch.

After Morgan entered Sean's life, he quit school for a semester, stopped going out with his friends because she wouldn't let him (even though she posted plenty of Facebook photos of her going out with her friends), and his common sense went out the window. At this time I was long over Sean, but as his friend, I knew Morgan was not good for him. Sean and Morgan broke up for a while, and when they got back together I lost all respect for Sean. I thought he knew better. We stopped talking for about six months, but I still woke up to plenty of "I miss you and I'm sorry" texts from him. I realized one day that even though I was annoyed with him, me not saying anything wasn't helping him move on, either. So we started talking once in a while again.

When I came back to school after studying abroad for a year, we hung out twice. And that's when shit really hit the fan.

I was doing homework when Morgan Facebook messaged me "How many times have you and Sean seen each other". Moments later Sean had me on speakerphone to tell Morgan that we did not have sex. After my friend of four years hung up on me, I replied to Morgan's Facebook message and gave her a piece of my mind. I realized that Sean's nerve to put his old friend's voice on the line right in between his pathetic relationship was enough of an indicator to know this friendship was no more. I haven't talked to Sean since.

It's easy to talk about Brad and Sean, because when they left my life they had douche bag status written all over them. But Carson is that one guy I want to talk about all the time, and yet don't want to let the world in on. He might read this, he might not, I don't know. But I do care. I always care when it comes to Carson.

I met Carson in seventh grade, and I knew I liked him the day I met him. I know; it was seventh grade and I really need to get over it. Trust me, I've told myself that. Even in seventh grade I knew I found a good one, and it made me feel crazy that I was head over heels for someone so young; but now I look back on that and I don't think I was crazy. Carson was and still is a guy *everyone* likes and respects. He's helpful, genuine, and just an all-around good person. And that's why I've never gotten over him. I've had moments in my life where I liked him more or less, moments where I liked other guys and thought something would transpire with them, but Carson never leaves my head...like I'm Forrest Gump accomplishing all these great things but I all I really want is Jenny. I think Carson notices me, but I don't know if I'll ever get to have him. So he continues to be a lingering what-if in the back of my head as I proceed on with my life.

Brad, Sean, and Carson are a component of my story...and that's kind of what I believe in, is the story of people's lives. I believe the story is always what it comes down to. It's a good story for me to call Brad and Sean losers after all the crap I went through with them. It's a great story to hope something might continue on with Carson. But some stories leave us happy at the end and some leave us disappointed. And some even leave us wondering.

My story is a process. It's constantly evolving. Sometimes it's really cheerful, and sometimes it's dramatic. Sometimes it's overly dramatic. It's also often times filled with fairy dust details of pictures I have in my head from memories of insignificant details, and yet those details are the key components to each layer of my tale. And sometimes it just is what it is.

What so often creates stories is the fact that we look forward at the big picture, and we look back at the little moments. Everybody wants to have a good tale to tell around the campfire, to joke about on a first date, or to share with their grandchildren one day. We all want to have a notable story that deserves a TED Talk, to be written into a screenplay, or to be the inspiration for our careers. At the end of the day, everything is your story; whether you did something, or whether you did nothing. How you reacted or didn't react. What you said out loud or what you screamed in your head. Where you've been and where you've stayed. Who you know. Every little aspect and choice you've made is your story...do you like yours so far?

In school, we aren't really taught in this way that the overall life goal is to have a good story. I think the story of your life is what the big picture is all about. Our want for a good story often leads us to what we accomplish, but the story itself is often times about the people who matter most to us. People are part of the little moments, the times we look back on in our lives. People are a huge component of those in-between moments we catch ourselves living; I find it's usually *people* that we are thinking about when we're supposed to be listening to our teacher's lecture or walking to our next class. Those people are often people we find attractive or hope notice us. I wish we discussed this kind of stuff more in the classroom; because it's what *everyone's* thinking about. Students get so much information stuffed into their face about alcohol, drugs, and sex, but what about just discussing the ups and downs of dating and figuring out how to find the right person? Even though it's not really talked about in the classroom, relationships are important. We prepare students to start their life story in so many other ways, but we often forget that dating is a huge part of the big picture.

We look forward at the big picture, we look back at the little moments.

Back in the good old 1990s I played with Barbie dolls and princesses during my childhood years. I had a whole freaking neighborhood set up of Barbie houses, cars for each home, five zillion accessories scattered on the floor, along with enough Barbie, Ken, and Kelly dolls to complete each family unit, batteries not included. Barbie taught me how to decorate a home, and it gave me subliminal insight to what a home is supposed to be according to 1950.

While I busily set up Barbie homes in my hey days, I also watched Disney princess movies nonstop. Cinderella, Jasmine, Pocahontas, Mulan, Ariel, Sleeping Beauty, you name it; those VHS tapes were always rolling. So again, while I was setting up what I imagined as the perfect households of my Barbie and Ken neighborhood, my eyes were also sucking in the glory of fairy godmothers fighting to make dresses blue or pink, all in the name of true love's first kiss.

It isn't my life goal to stop little girls from playing with dolls or watching Disney princess movies, but I will agree that small things like toys contribute to creating that big picture we have in our heads of what life is supposed to be.

That interior designer bug I had when I was decorating my Barbie mansion and townhouse followed me into my elementary days. I was not your ordinary child running off the school bus to watch *Spongebob Squarepants* at 3:30: I was running into the living room because *Trading Spaces* started at 3:00 and I had already missed half of it. Some kids lived for *Rugrats*; I lived for *House Hunters* (HGTV was my jam back in the day). For me growing up, it was all about thinking toward the ten years ahead of me. I was never good at being a child; I always wanted to be "grown up," living out my career dreams. I remember sitting in my third grade desk chair thinking to myself while we learned our multiplication skills, *how in the world am I going to become a Trading Spaces designer? How am I going to reach my dream job?* I'm telling you, I was not a normal kid.

That weirdness continued into my teenage years. My interior designer dream died out but evolved into Food Network cake decorator, and then Hollywood fashion stylist. I never aimed for normalcy in my life dreams; however I continued to plan out that big picture I had in my head of a career. But then I got to college, and I realized that it's really hard to plan the next ten years when you don't even know who you will be in one year.

The one thing I never planned out while growing up was college. In all honesty, I don't think I ever really wanted to go to college. I never thought about it, until it was time to decide where I was going to go to school. I had a dream school, but it was expensive. At the time I wanted fashion, but I wasn't entirely sure how to get to *Vogue*. So I went to a state school. It wasn't my dream school, but I made it work for me. This was all partially because the only thing I ever imagined was the big picture of my life; the moment of success, not the work it took to get there, and let's be real; we ain't all got the money to go to Harvard.

I've often heard women talk about this "fairytale" that they've always believed in, whether that fairytale is in love or in their professional lives. I don't really believe in fairytales, and I'm not even sure if I believe in the idea of chasing after your dreams. But I definitely am for taking action towards goals, and that's what life is entirely. It is the next step in going after whatever it is you want, whether that's a career or a spouse, and I try to do that with my own projects that are separate from what I've learned in the classroom. I always keep in mind that little girl who sat in her third grade desk dreaming of a big life, but now I work hard so I can say that little girl made it happen.

However, these days I'm old enough where lots of people my age are getting married and having babies. My Facebook feed is flooded with engagement photos, wedding rings, and pregnancy announcements literally everyday (while I've never once changed my relationship status from something other than single). And it makes me realize no matter how old you get, there's always something there reminding you about the big picture in life. Fifteen years ago my Barbie dolls and Disney princess love made me focus on the big picture; today Facebook and Pinterest make me think about it. The fairytale, the happily ever after, whatever you call it; we all think about the dream life we're intending to have. But then one day life hits you in the face with a bad test grade, a good guy you could seriously consider yourself marrying, or a positive pregnancy test. Either everything changes, or things go exactly as you were hoping. And you start asking yourself, "Is this *really* the life I imagined for myself?"

In life we look forward at the big picture, but we look back at the little moments. We don't think about all the work it will actually take to win the Oscar award or to give our TED Talk. We don't picture the effort before and after the wedding day that is required to sustain a strong romantic relationship with someone. But when we finally do reach those big moments we've been waiting for, we no longer know what to say when we get on stage to accept the award, or when we're crying off all our mascara to say our vows properly. Instead we flash back to all the little moments that got us to the stage or the altar, all the people we needed to meet to reach achievement. We think back to the laughs we had when we were living in a shitty apartment, or how thankful we now are that we didn't bail on that first date. When we're at the big picture moment, we refer to the little moments for comfort and a reminder of why we deserve this triumph.

So that makes the little moments of life very necessary. The small components of every day life are what build who we are as a whole. So if you want to have a damn good Oscar speech or most viewed TED Talk, if you want your wedding day to be epic, you've got to start with the development of yourself. It doesn't matter if you're chasing after a person or a job; knowing who you are will lead you to a life you want and the people you want in it.

One of the little moments I always think about in my life is the constant thought I had in my head as a teenager of wanting a boyfriend. I didn't always let it on to people, but I wanted to be in a relationship so badly. When I think about that want for a relationship, my mind instantly goes to the high school hallways in between classes, whether it was walking into school in the morning, going down the stairs, or just trying not to look like an idiot if I walked past a group of guys. And that vision of the busy hallway for three minutes between each class made me realize that you can't look down a high school hallway and expect to find your husband. What I mean by this is you can't wake up everyday, go to school, and walk around each corner wondering if your person is going to just run into you. You can't focus so much on searching for your person; you have to focus on searching for *yourself.*

Figure out yourself before you figure out someone else.

In the middle of the summer after our freshman year of college, my friend Rachel decided to drive up and meet me for lunch. I was really looking forward to hearing how life had been going for her since we'd last seen each other at the end of the semester in May. Rachel, to say the least, is very open about all occurring events in her life.

Rachel deals with personal anxieties that often affect her everyday life, and she's always been open about it with me. When we met at the beginning of our first year in college she explained to me that it caused her to graduate a semester later, and I watched her deal with it much of the school year. However, the way in which I would anticipate someone handling melancholies and stress was different from how Rachel handled her hardships throughout freshman year. I would expect someone to push themselves to attend scheduled events and classes, but Rachel skipped many classes and plans we made for lunch. I would presume that most people who have to cry would do it in private, but Rachel often did not. The first time I saw her breakdown she was crying and screaming in the middle of her kitchen, and it was something I've only seen children do. It was then that I realized as nice as Rachel is, she's got a lot of emotional matters. She "takes everything personally," as she once told me, and I feel it affects how she goes about life. She is very good at seeking out help when she has a problem, but that's just it; she has been treated like a princess her entire life, though I think she's aware of this. Rachel is extremely dependent on her parents, her roommate, and a boyfriend when she has one, and unless she has one of these crutches, she doesn't know how to hold it together with everyday life obstacles.

I felt after enduring our first year on our own together that Rachel had made a lot of progress towards becoming more like an adult. She was able to navigate her way to destinations, she was becoming a better communicator with professionals, and things were starting to become steady in her life. That all changed though after we parted ways the end of the year in May.

I asked Rachel how life was back home that day at lunch.

I've been fighting with my mom a lot," Rachel told me. I knew she was having arguments with her mom right before the school year ended. "It really comes down to the fact that she's trying to get me to grow up and I just don't want to," she said with a small laugh. "Like last Friday we were supposed to get my phone checked out by our service provider, and we were going to be there at nine thirty in the morning, but I didn't get up in time so she got really mad at me. And then we get in these arguments because she says she can't do everything for me anymore, and it's just really annoying."

"What about work; how's that going?" I asked.

"Ha, about that," Rachel replied, "I'm not even sure

if I still work there anymore…about a month ago I had a really rough night and I woke up still miserable and I just thought, *I cannot go to work today.* So I called up my boss and told her, "I'm so sorry, but I can't come in today, I'm just not up to it," and later on I put my two weeks notice in because of the same things, but my boss said she'll keep me on the schedule once a month and see where things go from there."

I'm not sure if it's just my hardcore work ethic or what, but this is why I don't pat Rachel on the back and say, "It's okay." I wish some people could sit in someone else's place and hear what comes out of their own mouths. I personally just do not have sympathy for people who give up without a definitive reason. Everyone has hard moments where they'd rather crawl into bed than go to work, but that's not how life goes. After she told me about her mother and work, Rachel started into her love life.

"So I decided to open up my profile again online," Rachel said, knowing that I was going to be judging this whole situation as she told it to me. This profile was on a dating website. When we were in school together, she met a guy from Georgia on this website and he flew cross-country to meet her during winter break. Things ended suddenly between them, and it left Rachel crushed. I told Rachel quickly after the end of that relationship no more Internet dating; she needed to learn how to connect with someone face to face.

"Oh God, Rachel," I said.

"….And I met someone, and we've been talking

since about June," she continued, "We've called each other, we've Skyped, we text…"

"Okay," I said, knowing there's got to be a catch to this whole thing.

"But guess where he's from," Rachel said, beaming, "Think of my favorite place."

"Georgia?" I answered, hoping to God we weren't going to go through that again.

"No."

"…California?"

"Nope."

Then it hit me, and some minor fury set in. "France."

Rachel smiled.

"Rachel, are you kidding me?!" I exclaimed.

It honestly started to get a little awkward. "And guess what his name is!" she said.

"I have no clue," I said, laughing at this point because that's all I could do.

"Philippe!"

I like Rachel, but sometimes I feel I am younger than her and more mature than she is. And that is something that left me very frustrated with our friendship and my social life in general while at college when I was having my own rough patches. I had much of myself figured out already. I was more stable emotionally, and even when I had a breakdown, I knew enough to go to the bathroom stall and cry it out rather than to bawl in front of God and everyone. I understand that nobody is perfect, myself included, but Rachel worries me sometimes with how up and down she can be emotionally.

It honestly made me slightly mad that Rachel started talking to this French boy Philippe. After everything she went through with the other online guy, after how sad she was that she could never see him because he was across the country, she now thinks she should try to be in a relationship with a guy who speaks a different language and lives across the pond in another country?! Didn't we learn how this works with the last guy?!

Rachel is still very much working to figure out herself and her own needs. Whether or not her emotional dilemmas are little issues or something bigger, I would like to know what it is that makes her think she can figure someone else out amongst all her own problems.

It's obvious why people search and go into relationships; we hope that someone else in this world might potentially be able to solve our issues, or if nothing else, help us escape our baggage. However, many times the exact opposite happens. I'm not trying to be a negative Nancy, but if Rachel thinks that some guy on a screen is going to save her from the realities of her work schedule or her mom telling her to grow up, she's got another thing coming. Rachel needs to figure out her life before she tries to become a part of someone else's life; she's got to figure out what she wants for herself before she can figure all that out in another guy.

This next part is going to come off as if I'm really bragging about myself, but it is what it is. I feel that the one characteristic everyone mentions when they try to explain my personality is *Stacey knows who she is.*

I believe in both five-inch Christian Louboutins and Target. I believe photographs can say more than words, a CD is better than buying the album on iTunes, and magazines are meant to be in print, not on a touch screen. I'd rather spend hundreds of dollars on a concert ticket to see Bruno Mars with my sister than on a new dress. I believe in good conversation, hearty meals at the dinner table, dressing up for no reason, and the magic of the movies.

I believe in people and their dreams, but I don't feel people understand the difference between dreams and goals. I don't think many people know what they want out of life, but I know what I want. I want cities and cinema; but I also want to help others, make a difference, and for people to hear my voice. I believe in God, but I also get mad at God. I also look forward to reading my horoscope every month. I want to be successful, but I don't need to be a millionaire. I want to travel and learn to appreciate the life I was given more and more everyday. I don't really want kids, but if I got pregnant at thirty-five, I'd be the happiest girl in the world. I can't tell you what we talked about in my classes today, but I can tell you what my friends and I talked about on the bus ride home from basketball games my sophomore year of high school. I pay attention to detail, and I remember every element in my memories. I will always believe in my golden high school class of sixty, I will forever love Taylor Swift no matter how many simplistic melodies she writes, I can't get enough of the Kardashians, and I think high heels are more comfortable than running shoes. I am a girly girl, but I also enjoy watching football, and I like walks in the woods.

I *do* know who I am.

I prize honesty, a desire to serve others, an ability to see beyond the surface area, and people keeping their word. I hope for my person to either be religious or to at least have enough faith to give God a chance. I want my person to have goals, a passion for what they're doing, and yes, I do hope they can help support both of us one day. I need someone who wants to travel and have adventures, because I need someone to teach me to loosen up more. However, I also need someone who feels like home. If my person isn't a virgin when I meet them I don't care. I don't even care if they smoke every now and then. I want my guy to be close with his family; if they don't want kids, that's okay, but they have to be close with their parents and siblings. They have to have a family that I hope to be part of one day. If they want a dog, fine, but no other pets (I have allergies).

I would not be able to state any of these personality traits or desires about myself had I not taken the time to focus on me, my wants, my needs, and my goals.

The biggest perk I am realizing more and more about being single for as long as I have been is that I get the blessing of figuring out who I am and who I want to become more than people who are in relationships. I do not donate the time that I spend immersed in my own interests trying to interpret someone else's life, and I'll be honest, I absolutely love that part of being single, and I think that's why it's good to be alone for periods of time. When you don't have someone texting you every two minutes or someone else's issues suppressed up against all yours, you have a lot of free time to examine yourself. You have the ability to fully concentrate on whatever it is you want to learn about, whether that's your talents, straightening out your life, or finding peace within yourself. Due to all the free time I've had in my years of aloneness, I know who I want to be, I know what I love, but I'm learning how to put it all together. I have dreams that consist of things very opposite of my present, but like every kid in my generation, I want the best of both worlds. I have faith, and I have confidence and determination. I know what I can and can't handle, and I like getting out of my comfort zone. And because I know these things about myself, I have characteristics to consider when I date other people: are they religious, do they want kids, are they going to be able to pay the bills, are they selfish, or are they needy. That's why it's so essential to figure out yourself before you figure out someone else. You have to be able to define your personality and your own needs, and by being able to do that, you will then be able to figure out what characteristics you need your person to have. And I mean, c'mon; what doesn't sound fantastic about giving yourself some time to focus on nothing but *you*? Besides tall, dark, and handsome, most of us just vie for some "me" time, and being single is the epitome of that.

There is never a right or wrong time to stop and analyze who you are, but also note that high school and college are kind of the prime starting times to do so. Your teenage years and your twenty something's are for *you*; this is the time before marriage and kids that you have to be completely selfish. Adults expect you to be selfish because you're young, so take advantage of that, with reason. As they say, you only live once, but don't make the idea of YOLO only about sex, drugs, and rock 'n' roll. Make YOLO traveling, participating in community service projects, joining a club, or exercising. These years are the time when you're supposed to figure out what you want to do with the rest of your life. One thing I wish someone would have told me before starting college, and is something I now am trying to tell people younger than me, is you don't need to know what you want to do or major in at age eighteen; you just need to know what you're interested in, because that alone is enough to steer you in the right direction. However, if you don't even know that, you honestly won't get ahead of the game, and I think people often don't know their interests because they've spent their young years only thinking about a boyfriend or girlfriend. So spend your bountiful amount of time afterschool or in between classes instead seeking not *who* you like but *what* you like, whether that's music, economics, technology, science, whatever.

I'll let you in on a little secret about college and meeting people; the first thing people ask you is what's your name, and then they ask about what you do. We are all about our jobs or our college majors, and we find those things by first discovering what aspects of life we find fascinating.

I personally believe that the things you'll be interested in for the rest of your life are the things you were interested in your *first* years of life. I remember writing and binding computer paper to make books at six years old; writing has been that one thing I've always fully understood how to do. I think everyone sees the world in a different way too; when I look at a flower in a vase, I look at it as if I was deciding how to paint it on a canvas, whereas a person interested in math may view it as a series of dimensions. However, you can't view life a certain way unless you've given yourself time to discover it as such. Therefore you have to practice what you love. You have to study it.

This brings me back to my memories of searching for my husband in the high school hallways. The idea of looking down a hallway at people for three minutes in between each class and thinking *my guy is here, I have to find him* makes no sense. But what does make sense is using those three minutes to rush to a club meeting or your favorite class. Because there you'll be able to form opinions, and your interests will lead you to people who share those opinions, and then bigger and better places with even more people who share and live out those ideas…and probably then to someone who you could spend the rest of your life with.

I think there are so many clichés and facts we constantly hear about love, and yet many of us tend to ignore; which in the end, is why we mess things up. Adults are constantly telling kids to enjoy life, live for the moment, and to not rush growing up, and yet most of us don't listen. And that's why people like Rachel struggle to find balance amongst their own life and the life of their potential partner. I believe the reason adults always tell kids to slow down in life is so we give ourselves time to *think*; think about what we would really be happy doing our entire lives, figuring out what makes us tick, and discovering what's truly important to us. However, due to my own experience, in order to figure out those characteristics of ourselves, we need to take some time to be single; and not just time while we're thirteen years old. Perhaps taking time in our early twenties or hell, whenever we really need is the necessity. Therefore you have to figure out yourself before you try to figure out someone else. You have to know *you* before you can really get to know someone else, otherwise that person or even your own freaking mind could take you to a place you don't want to go with your life. You can survive being sixteen years old and still single, trust me, and you can even survive being twenty and still single. Once you know yourself, you can take on another person, but until then, worry about learning *you*.

Know the difference between your heart and your brain.

You may have read that last section and wondered what

interests, goals, career dreams, and knowing yourself has to do with relationships; but that's the thing, it has everything to do with relationships. It's the basis to finding and starting a good relationship. And then the details branch out from there.

The first weekend I came back home from college was my high school's homecoming. I sat with my best friends Andrea and Meredith. When Meredith came up to join in catching up on all our new collegiate lives, she immediately asked Andrea, "Have you talked to Lana?"

"Yea," Andrea said with some agony.

"How was she when she talked to you?" Meredith asked.

"She was just really stressed and upset. It sounded like she's going to do it tomorrow."

Lana was one of my friends in high school, but also someone who got what I had always wanted: Carson. Lana and Carson started dating at the beginning of my and Lana's junior year (Carson was a senior). I hadn't really been interested in anyone when they started dating, but it was extremely weird to know that Carson was with someone. However, as the year was coming to a close and Carson's graduation approached, I realized that he was about to leave my life too, and I started falling for him hard all over again. I had finally become decent friends with him, and he now knew me for *me*, not for what everyone else portrayed me as when I crushed on him in middle school. In Carson's big picture, he wants to be close to his family, a good father, and to have a beautiful marriage. Lana was the type of girl who fit the bill for that scenario.

The second night I was home for homecoming weekend Lana, Andrea, and I decided to drive over to the high school dance a little early to see Meredith before grand march. While we were waiting, that was when Lana said, "Just so you guys know, Carson and I broke up today."

Andrea and I looked at each other with sadness for Lana and replied, "We knew already, we just didn't want to bring it up because we know it was hard for you."

Lana started to tear up. "I just couldn't balance everything. He constantly would want to come visit me on weekends, and if I told him I would text him after hanging out with my friends, he would constantly check up on me. I couldn't handle it anymore."

My jealousy for Carson was long gone by this point in our lives, but I did feel badly for both Lana and Carson. I hated thinking Carson was heartbroken, because I'm sure he pictured Lana being with him forever. But I understood what Lana was saying. Balancing a relationship with college has got to be extremely difficult; I don't know how anyone can master creating lifestyles in two different places at once for the person they love and for themselves. However, I do feel Lana is the one who lost out on someone special. Carson treated her like a queen; she was his whole world.

I think balance is like a math problem with an undefined answer, and love itself will always be uncertain because it's a feeling, not a fact. I often wonder if I can't prove love, will it ever work out?

I never had balance in high school. I was so busy with leading every freaking club, my job at a movie theatre, and my classes, that I instead voided out all the insanity and just got through it. But then when everything was completed, I would have an anxiety attack. I didn't know how to balance working with living life, but I believed so much in the race to success that I ignored any negative feelings I was enduring. And because of that, I came crashing down mentally and emotionally the summer before I came to college. I had finally gotten through all the emotions of realizing I was never going to spend another day of my life in high school, and then it hit me that I had to figure out how to handle the transition of leaving home and going to college. It made me realize how much my family means to me, as well as how much work it's actually going to take to get where I want to be in the career I've dreamt up in my head.

This career that I keep talking about is the only thing that I've thought about for almost my whole life; not how many kids I want, not the color of my dream house, *my career*. However, being twenty-something and still single has been making me evaluate balance a little more. Is it wrong to put so much emphasis on a career? They say a career doesn't love you back, but I don't want to settle for anything less. I've always been a career girl, but what if I still want to find my person?

In the history of human kind we've never seen so many people fail at relationships and marriage. However, people have more opportunities now than ever before to do whatever we want with our lives. We are allowed to travel the world, we can go to college, we can move to more urban areas, and we can do these things no matter our gender or race. With that said, we have more opportunity than ever before to *avoid* settling down, and often when people do settle down, they still feel they didn't accomplish all they wanted to do back when all they had to worry about was themselves. We can make life all about us if we want to. We can have plenty of sex without having any children. We welcome the idea of making business our main priorities; so where does love lie in between all that? My answer is between your heart and your brain.

There has to be some place in the human body that backs our reasoning and choices we make; choices such as when to stay or when to go in relationships. Everyone knows what I'm talking about here; that moment when you stop and think *ehh, do I really want to be with this person,* or that instant when a couple on the rocks is giving each other ultimatums to either continue being together or to throw in the towel. I think unfortunately every person is going to be faced with this kind of situation at some point with love. And this is why so many couples are in unhappy relationships—because they listen to their heart over their brain in circumstances where they might potentially end up heartbroken.

As I explain the difference amongst what your brain tells you and what your heart tells you, I'm going to use my story with Brad to evaluate what I mean. To give you a refresher, Brad is the guy who I attempted to date on and off again for two years. After things ended first semester of college, Brad and I started talking again second semester of my freshman year. I continued to be moderately hopeful in that we would really start dating, as I was a naïve nineteen-year-old, very willing to give him a second chance. But once again, things got rocky with Brad, and spoiler alert; we quit talking because of it for some time.

So this is my *heart* telling you what happened second semester with Brad and I:

As I was moving back into the groove of college my second semester, Brad and I started talking again. But for some reason I'm still trying to figure out, Brad and I just faded like we had before. We both became busy, and we went from talking everyday to a text here and there. And then nothing. And then I kind of called him out about it. I told him I didn't know what to think when we went so long without talking; I didn't know if I did something wrong, and it made me freak out inside, and I didn't want him to know that because I didn't want to come off as a crazy psycho, but I also had to be honest because that's what I believe in.

I was too scared to ever ask Brad to hang out, or to ask what happened to us, and I don't know why we didn't work out, again. I don't know why God brought him into my life just to take him away for a second time. His interests were different from mine, but I was willing to take those differences into consideration; and those differences made him that much more interesting to me.

Brad is a well-rounded individual, and to me, he's the whole package. Brad's values reinforced mine, his lifestyle intrigued me, and his personality made me feel like I was a middle school girl crushing on the cutest boy in my class. He set the bar high, and all I can think after knowing him is God must have an amazing guy in store for me, because I don't know how He'll ever top this one. I don't blame Brad for being unable to balance a potential relationship and everything he had going on with school; but then why did he come around for a second time? If he knew he didn't have time the first try then why did he want to give it another go?

Aaaannndd this is my *brain* telling you what happened with Brad and I:

Once second semester started, Brad would message me every couple weeks. We would have great conversations about basically anything and everything, and finally we started hanging out again. I was so excited that maybe, just maybe, I might have a potential new man in my life. But then shit hit the fan again. Suddenly, no texts. No more hanging out. I honestly felt at times like Brad was trying to cut me out of his life, so I told him that I didn't know what to think with this weird off-and-on thing. I still think I fucked it up by saying this, but I also think Brad didn't do his part in being a team player. No, we were not official, but in order to keep a person of interest in the loop, you've got to hold up your end of the bargain. And my God, was it a sin for me to feel that Brad should chase me if he wanted a second go-around at whatever this was with me?

I couldn't bear to hear him say again, "I don't have time to date right now," because that phrase doesn't mean he doesn't like me. It means we're going to run in circles all over again a month from now, like we just had a month prior. I would rather hear Brad say, "I don't have feelings for you" instead of "I don't have time to date."

In this scenario, balance isn't what stopped Brad and me from becoming more than friends. *My* loss of balance between what my heart and my brain was telling me is what caused me some minor heartbreak in the dead of winter that second semester.

There's something I realized with this whole up-and-down whirlwind with Brad, and it's that there's a major difference between your heart and your brain. The worst moments for me after Brad and I basically quit talking were from 8 P.M. to 11 P.M., because that was the time when I expected to hear from Brad; and part of me for a while after still hoped his name would pop up on my phone. That though was when my heart was speaking louder than my brain. The miserable week I encountered at the end of February realizing that Brad was not going to commit to anything more was when my brain started doing the talking. My brain can be like Kourtney Kardashian talking shit about her boyfriend Scott Disick; the same voice, with the same inflections of carelessness, anger, and over-it attitude. But my heart speaks when it's quiet; when I'm trying to fall asleep, always when I wake up, and when I looked at the clock at midnight and knew that I wouldn't hear from Brad that night. My heart asked the questions like *Why did God bring Brad into my life?* and my brain told me *You deserve someone who is head over heels for you.* My brain certainly did more talking the second time around while moving on from Brad; I think the first time we didn't work out strengthened my brain's voice. My heart is my emotions, and my brain is the truth.

I believe now, after Brad, and after seeing couples like Lana and Carson, that balance isn't making room for someone in your life, but rather it is knowing the difference between what your heart tells you and what your brain tells you. Like I said before, love is a feeling, not a fact, and you have to remember that if you realize you or someone else isn't putting in enough commitment to your relationship. The red flags that come up when you're developing a relationship with a person is your brain speaking to you, so listen to it. Yes the truth hurts, but the sooner you listen to your brain, the better off you'll be. I absolutely hate the quote "Follow your heart"; first of all it's so trite it makes me want to vomit, but it's such a trap into leading people to be emotionally distressed. Listening to your heart in difficult circumstances like break-ups will never help you move on, it'll just make the mess drag on, and I've figured out that the people who do "follow their heart" are the ones who don't go far in life, because they take everything personally. Your brain's voice should never turn off in a relationship, from the moment you meet each other till death do you part. If Lana hadn't listened to her brain saying she couldn't handle being a college student and a girlfriend to Carson, she would've gone crazy. I know she hated breaking Carson's heart, but she needed to do what was best for her at that point in her life. I'm still not sure what the hell Brad listens to; maybe it's his heart, then his brain, or both, or alcohol, or his dick. That sounds mean, I know, but that's just what *my* brain's saying at this point. However, my heart is saying that I was finally starting to feel steadiness in my life with Brad around. I was learning to put the homework away at nine o'clock and giving myself time to relax. I was starting to realize that maybe there's a reason people try so hard to make a career and a relationship last both equally and successfully. And amongst all that, my heart *and* my brain were saying that I would've been a fantastic girlfriend to him. I would've been perfectly happy if we only hung out once a week and then texted in between, because that would have still showed me that he cared and was willing to balance his interest for me with everything else in his life. His brain would have continued being logical while his heart told me he cared.

There's a difference between a "thing" and a "relationship."

Let's clarify something here while we're talking about the heart and the brain; these two body parts have a hard time distinguishing what a "thing" is with someone and a "relationship" is with someone.

A relationship is when two people have officially said to society, whether it's introducing someone as a boyfriend or girlfriend at a party or a life event on Facebook, that they will be hanging out regularly, possibly showing some P.D.A. from time to time, taking really basic pictures together for Instagram, and gradually start looking like each other, all because they legitimately care for one another.

A "thing" with someone ranges from someone you text regularly and tell all your deep dark secrets, to a friend-with-benefits. This person probably won't take basic Instagram pictures with you, depending on their personality they may show you off to their friends from time to time, but you will definitely not be in any profile picture with them. So a "thing" is *similar* to a relationship, but the definite difference is that you will *not* be announcing to the world that you are in a relationship, because you are not. Symptoms of a "thing" include one person getting really pissed off and confused while the other is in la-la land, heavily avoiding the word 'relationship'. The pissed and confused one will often ask, "What are we?" while the other will dodge the question all together. If you are interested in romantically dating someone and the pattern of likeness is constantly up and down, you may be in a "thing" with someone.

I was in a "thing" with Brad. My heart and my brain could not differentiate if this guy was worth it or not. So eventually time showed me I needed to move on.

When I liked Brad, I always worried I would lose my balance, but then I realized that I never really had balance in the first place. When we started to fade away, I lost steadiness again. My anger came back, and I was pleading for my work to take my focus away from everything in my love life. I had been left with the feeling of knowing I had someone good, but never having been allowed all of him. I realized that nothing is guaranteed in this life; love, career success, happiness, financial support, and especially balance. But that's why you keep going in life. That's why your brain tells you to keep moving forward, and it's why I've kept on keeping on during these singular years.

But then I thought to myself, *what the fuck am I doing worrying about this guy?* He didn't bring anything that great to my life. He made the big picture of my life feel closer to me than it really was; but he certainly didn't fit into it. Now when I look back at the times I was somewhat unsure about Brad, I'm not in love with any of those little moments. I'm thankful they happened because I learned a lot, but Brad and I were nowhere near relationship status, ever.

I can't tell you how to balance your life, but I truly believe it starts with figuring out who you are as an individual, understanding that your heart talks differently from your brain, and then maybe that can help decipher if the guy or girl you like makes you a pissed and confused son of a gun or a better person. Learning about yourself first will help you observe what people in this world have yet to do so for themselves, and you will find that the people who do try to get themselves together are often times the ones ready to be in a relationship and not a "thing."

*

Most authors don't discuss the major plot line of a story until the end of the book, but when it comes to relationships, I don't think we should save the most important aspect of dating and love till the end; that's what leads to bad break-ups and divorces. So the biggest, most important, major idea I've learned from never having a boyfriend is that everything is your story. Everything you do, your interests, the people you surround yourself with; those things compile and create who you are. So you have to ask yourself...what do you want your story to be? Relationships don't start with another person; they start with *you*. In order to develop a strong bond with a boyfriend or girlfriend, you have to know who you are, otherwise there's going to be some awkward silence either on that first date, or ten years down the road when you realize you don't know who you are in this relationship you're in.

My story, like I said, is constantly evolving. The story of our lives is never completely finished, but it definitely is started, so to be able to establish what you'd like your big picture to be, you have to have little moments to look back on. That means you need interests, hobbies, and a personality to show someone how freaking fantastic you are. I often find that people who constantly hop from relationship to relationship (or from "thing" to "thing") are people who haven't taken time to look inside themselves and, as cliché as it sounds, discover who they are. It is worth everything to spend some time perhaps dating yourself. If you give yourself time to do something *you* want to do, travel to a place *you* want to see, or set a goal for *yourself*, you really will learn more about who you are. Good looks and sorority picture poses get old after a while…at some point, people want to sit down with you and get to know *you*. So go to a movie by yourself, walk through a museum alone, start running; figure out yourself before you figure out someone else. And as you learn more about who you are and where you want to go, you'll become more confident in distinguishing your heart from your brain. This is so crucial in life, because no matter how confident you are in yourself, you will always come across some absolute losers who somehow manage to walk this earth. You gotta dodge the dummies from the good ones; know when someone's mature enough for a relationship and not just a "thing."

A story is very detailed, and yours is no different. You'll have many drafts, times when you don't know where to go next with a character or moments when you're disappointed with an outcome. But you were given the chance to have a great story, so be brave enough to look into the details of your identity to write a classic.

DRAFT YOUR IDENTITY

In my own experience trekking through life, I have found that our soul is who we are, our heart picks the dream, and our brain goes after the goal. So in order for the soul, heart, and brain to work together, you have to discover yourself, love every part of you, and then go find someone who will love you just as much.

As you're working to figure out yourself, you are truly soul searching. When you find that one thing that you know you're good at, be it music, farming, cooking, fashion, whatever, you know in your soul that is the subject matter you are going to be a genius at. That is what figuring yourself out is all about. You're learning what you can and can't handle, what makes you tick, what gets you excited, your weaknesses and your strengths. Knowing those details about yourself is what will make you stand out from other people; it's so obvious in people's personas and their walk when they know who they are. There's a certain self-assurance they have with each step and the way they look at people. That's a confidence factor someone has found within their soul;

when you know who you are, you know what you want; and it will become natural for you to show that off to the world.

While your heart and your brain bring together two very different components of your identity, they both supply very necessary tools to create your big picture. The brain brings knowledge and skills...the stuff you'll need to actually accomplish a task. Your heart though is exactly that– your *heart*. It's your emotions and motivation that you bring to whatever you do; it's your feelings for someone. Success is only possible if you have both your heart and your brain in check with what jobs they're supposed to do to help your soul's passion come alive. So the heart and brain are a part of developing who you want to be, and they both really do need to be tested by society and heartbreakers to become strong. Your heart and your brain have everything to do with why some days you feel great about yourself and some days you hate your life. It's the reason we can go from silly stupid happy to pissed off crazy in .02 seconds. However, it's no one else's job to manage your heart and your brain, not even your significant other's job. It's all up to you to know how to separate the facts of life from your emotions, and when it's necessary to do so.

My brain has taught me don't major in husbandry; my heart has taught me to love yourself.

Stacey Springob

Don't major in husbandry.

Throughout my first year at college I sold tickets at athletic events. One night I was working with my coworker Ronny, when a man who was probably around seventy years old walks in with his ticket, ready for me to stamp his hand. There was plenty of time before the game started and we weren't busy selling tickets, so this man started asking us about our lives, as many people like to do with college students.

"So you kids go here for school?" said the old man.

"Yes, we do sir," replied Ronny.

"What are you both majors in?" he asked.

Ronny simply stated, "Business Administration," something anyone of any age could easily understand.

But try telling a seventy-year-old man whom you've just met what the hell "Professional Communication and Emerging Media" is.

"It's basically a journalism degree," I said.

"Journalism?" the man skeptically replied, "What are you going to do with *that?* How are you going to make any money with that degree?"

"Well, there's a lot of need for people to run social media sites for businesses and keep website entries up to date," I said, knowing this guy had already made up his mind about my future endeavors.

"How do you expect to get a job in that?" he said.

Once again, I said the same thing in a different way. But it's what he said next that blew my mind.

"Hmm. Well you're probably really *majoring in husbandry.*"

I was so taken aback; I just laughed it off and agreed as the asshole walked away. I should've told him I was a lesbian.

I know today we really live in a Beyoncé bow-down-bitches-who-run-the-world-girls society, but it really is each person's job, boy or girl, to show others your worth in this world. No one is ever going to hand you anything in life, unless you put in the work. And it really doesn't matter where you come from; at this point in the game, too many people have shown society that you can come from nothing and become someone. After that old man said I'm "majoring in husbandry," my perspective in showing anybody who will listen my worth became incredibly important to me; so much that I even try to get the attention of people who don't want to listen.

I grew up in small town USA; Wisconsin to be exact. My hometown has less than two thousand people in it, and my high school class was a group of sixty kids who started kindergarten at one end of the building and graduated thirteen years later together at the other end. I truly grew up in a place comparable to something out of the 1950s. My childhood was every lyric on country radio; everyone knows everyone, and people get married young. Like, *young.* Like as in one-tenth of my classmates are already hitched (and then you have me who's never been in a relationship). By the time I graduated high school, I knew seven teen mothers from various grades.

It is extremely common for people in my area to marry their high school sweetheart and never leave town. And there truly is nothing wrong with that; I believe some people are relationship people and some people are career people. I want a big career, but some people dream of being a mommy or daddy like I dream of being a New Yorker. But I also think there are plenty of people who just follow this pattern of settling down before establishing a career because it's all they know– and that's what I was always against when I was growing up in small town USA.

I grew up in a good home. My parents are very loving of me, and my sister is my best friend. My family is very spread out all over the country, so that worked to my advantage in that I got to travel a lot as a kid. I was able to see palm trees instead of pines, Spanish style homes instead of log cabins, and mountains rather than dairy farms. Along with that, I was exposed to the fact that people have different lifestyles from one another. I got everything I ever wanted as a child, but with reason. I learned how to save my own money for things I wanted. But I was also shown that hard work could earn you expensive houses, an enjoyable city lifestyle, designer clothing, and nice cars. Growing up I saw with my own eyes the material items I could have if I worked hard, but it was the exposure to the idea of something beyond small town Wisconsin that I am extremely grateful for today. A lot of kids I grew up with were lucky if they got to visit Disney World once. Seeing Chicago is a big deal to most small town Wisconsin folks, who only live a state away.

A lot of people don't ever get out in small towns, and that's all I ever wanted to do growing up; because I knew there was more out there. I was fortunate in that I had a chance to see life outside my comfort zone starting from a young age, and that opportunity kept me eager to do more with my life.

So when some asshole told *me*, the girl who's after everything *besides* being a wife at eighteen, to major in husbandry, that's when a flip switched in my brain. Let's get one thing straight here; I don't fucking major in husbandry. I am career girl, the one who makes shit happen! And that's why your brain works the way it does; to tell things to you straight when you need it. Your brain is there to signal "Asshole at three o'clock," meaning it will be the thing inside you saying, "This person is wrong and I am capable of being more than they size me down to," or it's there to say "Wake up and get your shit together!" when you're being lazy and dumb.

In most circumstances, I am way better at listening to my brain than I am to my heart, because I talk more like my brain on a regular basis. I have a toughness in my soul that the brain also holds. My parents growing up didn't solve my problems for me; if I had an issue with someone, I stood up for myself. And in my household, we give each other a lot of crap, and we're very blunt with one another (while loving at the same time). I discipline myself today with the exact words my dad would use to discipline me as a kid. I like to think most fathers are similar to a Cliff Huxtable or Brady Bunch type; my dad is an Archie Bunker. To put this into perspective, rather than saying "You have to go do that yourself," my dad would say, "Get off your dead ass and do it yourself!" So this mantra and yet jokingly persona in our household is very much a part of my personality today, and I think it's very comparable to the way the brain works. The brain doesn't say "Turn off Netflix and do your homework," it says "Sit your ass down and get this shit DONE." So when we're talking about life, and going after something bigger than yourself, the brain is going to say "If you want the world, don't major in husbandry." And that is what I have learned as a woman, a young person, and someone with drive; don't major in husbandry.

When I say 'don't major in husbandry,' that doesn't mean don't get married and start a family one day, it means don't spend your young years so freaking focused on one person, spend that time practicing something you're interested in. Don't chase people when you're a teenager or a twenty-something; chase ideas, places, or goals. If your dream is to study abroad in Fiji for a semester, don't decide against it because you fear you'll miss your boyfriend back home too much. If your significant other really loves you, they'll support you in doing something exciting with your young years. If you grew up in Iowa but you want to become a hot shot in New York, you can absolutely do that. I don't believe that *anything* is possible in life, but I know that you can work your ass off for something you want more than anything and either make it happen, or find something even better. You can go to college even if you can't afford it; it might take two jobs while you're in school, it might take longer than four years to complete, but you can get a degree rather than work at your high school job for fifty more years.

When you're eighteen, the world seems so big, and guess what? It is. So give yourself a chance to experience it, to really make a name for yourself. Don't major in husbandry; listen to your brain when it says, "You are capable of more" or "You are being stupid, go do something valuable with your time". Allow yourself the opportunity to set a goal, brainstorm how to make it a reality, and do everything in your power to make it your life. You can only gain something from an experience like that. I think a lot of those people who do major in husbandry worry they won't reach a certain checkpoint in their lives if they fail at their goals, but you seriously cannot fail. If something doesn't work out, you'll figure out another way to go, because that's the thing; you *have* to figure out another way. You can't just give up on yourself. No one is going to reach out a hand to you if you just sit there and never give life a shot. Some people like me are fortunate enough to see that there's more out there than our hometowns, and others are smart enough to believe there is something bigger. Don't major in husbandry, and don't stop yourself from actually proving you can create a life *you* want rather than one you're just familiar with.

Stacey Springob

Be a man.

While the idea of 'don't major in husbandry' applies to both females and males, I will admit when I discuss it I tend to think of it more towards females. This is simply because I grew up with so many girls who were more than willing to settle down with a guy before ever seeking out her own ambitions, and more times than not the guy was a complete idiot. I hope those girls who never take time to be single or may be going farther with a guy than they actually want to right now take the idea of 'don't major in husbandry' into serious consideration. That said, males can also relate to the majoring in husbandry idea…plus, one more thing.

Boys, let's make one thing real clear here…the way to a woman's heart is chivalry. Seriously. So yes, flowers, chocolate, paying attention to what your girl likes and surprising her with that crap every once in a while, that is necessary. You will separate yourselves from the sea of boys in a snap, I promise, because chivalry (good manners, class, respect) proves you are a man. Ask a girl to prom in person, tell her she looks pretty, text her good night with a smiley face; she is waiting for you to do so! Man up and show her you're brave.

I love the male gender, and I'm rooting for them as much as I root for the ladies, but as a female, I notice how much media is out there about all the things women do to prove their worth. From college, to the workplace, to the bedroom, to motherhood, to how much food we put on our plates at Christmas, there is so much crap out there being discussed and overanalyzed about how women should be. There is *nothing* out there being discussed at this level for men. So guys, I'm simply saying, whether you're a gentleman or you're a dumbass, think about how often women are showing in the press that they are just as high up as men, and realize how much of that you *don't* have to do as a male. You automatically get a kind of respect that women have been working to earn for a ridiculous amount of time. I get so annoyed when I see guys sit on their asses, not doing anything with their lives, and then I see girls working their butts off, proving they can be just as awesome as guys. If you say you're a man, then be a fucking man, especially to your girl; it's just common sense.

Ladies, stop obsessing about your weight!

I. Am. So. Sick. Of. Skinny. Bitches. Complaining. About. Their. Weight.

If you are five hundred pounds, then yes, perhaps you should look into losing some weight. But if you are a size ten or smaller, shut up! Guys don't notice that shit, seriously. Nobody has time to decide if your left thigh is bigger than your right, if you have more arm flab than you had last week, or if your tummy falls over your pants by half an inch when you're sitting down. If you are naked in front of a guy, if you are walking around in a bikini in front of the male species, he is not concerned about the fat of your inner thighs, okay? If you are a size six or smaller, if you are one of those crazy bitches who 'loves working out' and you eat apples and oranges for fun, guess what? You will NEVER be fat. You will not let yourself get to that point, ever. One cookie does not make you blow up (trust me even two, three, four, or even five cookies will not make you blow up, according to my taste testings). Everybody gets double chin when they look down and everyone has a food baby after dinner. The people who freak out about being fat are never fat, so NO YOU'RE NOT FAT. Now go eat a puff pastry because you can.

There is nothing wrong with being confident.

We hear our parents and elders always saying not to worry about the haters, and as much as I rolled my eyes about it when I was a teenager, I say the same exact thing to my sister now. Screw the haters, seriously…not just because they're probably bitches, but also because you don't have time to worry about them if you're giving yourself the focus of learning about yourself. Those losers aren't going to get it; they just aren't. But you're not learning about yourself to impress them, anyways.

I was always really good at drawing and painting in

school, and many times I'd be halfway done with my project in art class and people would be able to see the piece coming together. And mind you, my artwork always looked good. There would always be one kid who would look at my work and yell "WHOA Stacey that's so good!" And then everyone would come over and admire my work while I was in the process of being awesome. Part of me loved those moments, and part of me hated those moments. Who doesn't love attention, but at the same time who wants all the attention on them, you know? I was just doing something I was good at, and I was doing a damn good job at it. So I was confident about it, and whenever I finish a project I'm proud of, I continue to show off my confidence in my work. And there is nothing cocky about that. If someone is confident about something they didn't put any effort into, then yes, they're being cocky and annoying. But if you've put the time, blood, sweat, and tears into something, you are more than allowed to be confident in presenting that final result to your peers.

Confidence really is something few people have, and we emulate the few people we notice who do have it. You always remember the person in the room who showed confidence, whether you loved or hated them. The confident person doesn't give a shit what anybody thinks, because they don't need to. They have worked to prove themselves to the crowd they're trying to please. So keep that in mind as you grow and develop more into the person you want to be.

One of the reasons I first noticed Brad was because I

was attracted to his confidence. We met in our speech class, and towards the end of the semester, I decided I was going to somehow get this guy who sat behind me to notice me. I offered him the speech topic I originally wanted to use once I thought of a better idea, and when class time arrived and Brad was up next, he nailed his speech. As cheesy as I might sound, Brad's passion for life completely shined through as he told us all why we should travel. I sat there during his speech, honest to God, thinking *Fuck, I like him.*

While Brad got my attention by being confident, I think the same went for when I caught his eye. Next class it was my turn to talk about why everyone should "find their happy." I don't know why, but when I get to talk about something that's supposed to be inspirational or motivational towards my audience, I get super nervous. Showing confidence doesn't always necessarily mean you feel confident in the moment; sometimes you gotta fake it till you make it. It's like that idea that 'fearless' doesn't mean you have no fear, it just means you have the courage to do something even though it might scare you. I had practiced this "finding happy" speech probably fifty times because I had to know it word for word in order to get my points across (I like to make things more complicated for myself so I can stand out, a surprise to many I'm sure), and even though I did know it, I still started blanking as I walked up to the front of the classroom. I had thirty words on a note card to help me remember, but that did nothing when I blanked in the middle of telling my speech class (and Brad) how to "find your happy." After about ten seconds I jumped back in and dominated the rest of the speech. While I was frustrated that I messed up, I was pretty sure I still did a good job and the point came across to my audience. But even when I was blanking, I didn't let go of my confidence.

After class I walked to the student center. As I walked in I saw Brad. He walked beside me suddenly and said "Hey, good job on your speech!"

"Thanks," I said trying to act cool, "you did really good on yours, too!"

I walked back to my dorm thinking *Well the most important person to me in that room liked my speech so I guess I accomplished what I wanted to do.* A couple days later I added him on Facebook, and a couple days after that he messaged me out of the blue! Even in my moment of fear in doing this speech, keeping my confidence in check paid off and got me a date with the cute guy from speech class.

I think confidence is something girls especially don't like to show too much of, mainly because we ladies fear other bitches will talk behind our back. Reality is that of course some bitch is gonna talk behind your back; some chicks have nothing better to do. But confidence is sexy. When a girl has high heels on, you know if she is feeling good about herself from her walk. She either rocks those heels or she looks like a dud walking in them. But confidence is what makes guys attracted to you; at least, what attracts the good guys. The guys who'll bring you roses and chocolate will notice confidence in a girl from a mile away; and they're mature enough to handle it.

The one thing that sucks about a confident lady is, I do truly believe, it often intimidates guys (And well it should!). As a single gal, I have never had a man to depend on. I'm very used to opening my own car door and paying my own bill at the restaurant, and what's even bigger is I'm used to drying my own tears when I'm stressed out about something. I'm well rehearsed in picking up the pieces myself. And I'll be very honest; I *don't* need a guy to depend on. I want a guy for company, to enjoy life with. I can take care of myself and I know how to make myself happy. At the end of the day, I really just need a good friend and a cuddle buddy when it comes to finding the right guy, because I've got my shit figured out for the most part. However, this doesn't sit well with all guys. A man's role has usually been to support the girl, to be the provider for the family; but I plan to provide for myself. I don't need a guy to make myself feel confident, but I still want someone next to me to enjoy the ride with. In that respect, a guy has to understand I've got the confidence part down, and just let me roll with it. This confidence discussion leads into one of my most important lessons from being single.

Love yourself.

I find it very ironic that we put more emphasis on age eighteen instead of age nineteen, because in reality, nineteen is one of the biggest years; no one happens to ever mention that little detail about life though until you're actually there. Eighteen obviously is a big deal because you're a senior in high school and you're the celebrity of your hometown, but age nineteen is the first year on your own, no matter what path you go down. That's a way bigger deal than anything going on at eighteen if you ask me. I think a lot of people can easily reminisce about when they were nineteen, simply because there's no way you can forget about all the 'firsts' of that one year. It's really great and really tough, and you experience a lot of emotions, but I think that time can also be what really drives us to find our purpose as we enter the next phase of life.

I wish I could tell you my freshman year of college was absolutely fantastic, but it wasn't. Honestly, it pretty much sucked ass up until the last three weeks. However, my first year out of high school truly did establish my most important thoughts and beliefs on love. I've discussed plenty of moments throughout this time but there is one part I haven't brought up yet, and that's the part where I started to find myself.

I was terrified to move to college. Even though all I ever dreamed about as a kid was getting out of my hometown, the moment it hit me that I was actually leaving home for some new life filled with God knows whom and what was scary as hell. The summer before I left for college was one of the worst times of my life, as I literally lived in fear everyday for the unknown of the future. I hated when people asked if I was excited, and I did everything I could to hold in the tears when I had to pretend to be happy about it. I cried the entire drive to freshman orientation and left it just as uncertain. At that time all I wanted was to be a fashion stylist, but finding success in fashion isn't like becoming a doctor or lawyer. Doctors go to medical school, lawyers go to law school, but you don't really even need a degree to be an expert in fashion. So where was I supposed to find a job in that? And the biggest question at that time for me was how the hell a state school in Wisconsin was ever going to get me to New York City.

The first month of college was great. I actually made friends, my roommate and I were getting along, and my classes weren't overwhelming like everyone told me they might be. I was surviving, and that's all I wanted after enduring my summer anxieties. But by the time second semester rolled around, I was realizing there was really little I enjoyed about my school. I was giving my all to my classes and extra-curricular activities. But I didn't have many friends, I was epically failing at any love life I attempted, and winter was absolutely deteriorating any happiness I still had. I was living alone in a jail cell of a dorm room because my roommate did not come back second semester. I struggled to find a place in fashion between sewing and retail that I thoroughly enjoyed, and I was beginning to wonder if my movie theatre days and love of TV production was where I was supposed to be instead. I was angry all the time, wondering if life was *ever* going to come together.

I am a person who tries to make the best of a bad

situation, because more times than not, life is still hard. I stayed busy at school, I didn't go home on weekends, and yet I wasn't enjoying this new chapter of my life; and I never truly believed that this school in another small town was going to get me to the major city life that I'd always dreamed. I was well aware of the fact that I was not finding my niche at school, so I looked into other options. I decided to take advantage of the study abroad program, so I applied to spend a semester in southern California and New York City for my sophomore year, and that decision truly put me on the right path.

Sometimes in life, you need another place to make you feel whole again. That's what I was searching for when I studied abroad. If I tell you all about my time away from home for a year I'll just sound like a privileged white girl. Just know it was everything Elizabeth Gilbert said in *Eat, Pray, Love* from the food, to the people, to the memories. Traveling for a year was epic and unforgettable, but for me personally it also gave me a chance to experience the places I want to be in my career one day. It allowed this small town girl to navigate the New York City subway system alone, and to ride the Pacific Coast Highway from L.A. to San Francisco. It also allowed this small town girl to give herself a chance at the life *she* wants. Studying abroad was fantastic and very terrifying, but it woke. me. up. I've always loved myself, but doing something for *me* put that love into action to start creating my big picture. That was something only I could give myself, not something a boyfriend could do for me.

In those dark moments during my freshman year, I sometimes wondered what it was I did wrong my first year in college that didn't allow me to make a lot of good friends right away. How could I have felt so alone when there are thousands of people walking all over that campus everyday? Was it because I didn't party on weekends? Was it because I didn't join a sorority? Is that *really* what I needed to do to become that girl with all those fabulous Facebook photos of me with my perfect, gorgeous college friends? And what about Brad; how come that didn't work out? I really thought he was going to be the boyfriend I brought home from college. How could it be possible that I was willing to be someone's everything and yet to Brad I was practically nothing?

A week before I was done with my first year of college, a thought about Brad passed through my mind, and it was at that moment when I rolled my eyes and realized I was finally over him. I was sick of debating him in my mind, what I could've done to make us work out, and I had finally come to my senses that I love myself too much to allow someone a third chance. *I am over him*, I thought to myself and also told God. And the next day I kid you not, Brad messaged me on Facebook. We'd barely said anything to one another for months, yet here I was *again*, moving on and getting held back. This time though I couldn't help but wonder whether or not it was God's intentions to bring Brad and I back together. I believe that sometimes people enter our lives not necessarily for us to learn from them, but vice versa. So I questioned if my call to God saying I was over Brad was answered by rewarding me with Brad, or by teaching Brad my value as a person in *his* life.

I figured out after this epiphany that distance is what screws us all up when it comes to love. I am always busy in college, but at that time my mind was just as busy getting over Brad. Every now and then I would run into him on campus, and it would just mess with me, almost serving as a trigger into making my mind run in circles. Sometimes I honestly feel like I have a disorder or something since I've never had a boyfriend, because it's this characteristic about myself that makes me unable to relate to a lot of people's circumstances, and it leaves me feeling extremely lonely at times. It's made me view the world in a different way compared to many of my peers. I was disappointed that things didn't work out between Brad and I, but I was also frustrated with the hopeless feeling I often have about ever meeting someone special. I was trying so damn hard to get over Brad, and literally every single time I was making progress, he would show up again in some way or another. The distance I had from him while I was trying to move on made me want him more, and when time eventually had me focusing on other parts of life, he'd slip back in.

The last Friday night that I was living in the dorms, I was on my computer at one thirty in the morning when Brad Facebook messaged me again. I expected it to be some lame small talk conversation, but exactly the opposite occurred. When Brad and I caught up with one another after a long period of time, we had fantastic conversations; but this conversation in particular made me feel that perhaps sometimes in life we should just appreciate a magical moment for what it is and leave it at that. When I least expected it, Brad apologized for the times he was a douche bag to me, and he admitted to his fear of commitment. We ended up talking until 3 A.M., and when I went to sleep that night I felt *closure*; something I never expected to receive with the whole Brad adventure. I had been content with the unanswered questions in my head and trying to fill in the gaps myself. While I still had no idea what to expect from then on knowing the patterns of my past with Brad, I was thankful in knowing that we were okay, and that I could trust in believing Brad is important enough to keep in my life even as just a friend.

I wish I could tell you that it ended there with Brad, and that I knew better than to give it another shot. But the Scorpio sign in me doesn't like to give up, and I let Brad in again. We kept up with each other's daily lives during the summer. I even drove out of my way to visit him when I was driving home from seeing another friend on the other side of the state. I started giving a shit again, even when I knew I could do better...a lot better.

But there I was sitting with Brad the week before I left for studying abroad in California at his friend Raymond's house, as Brad and Raymond conversed about the summer over a couple beers while I occasionally chimed in. Perhaps it was the Blue Moon in Brad's hand that got the ball rolling, as he told Raymond about all the girls he hit on this summer at the bars, right in front of me. Raymond tried to express a look of notification to Brad that I was in the room, knowing that Brad and I had some type of relationship above the level of friendship.

But Brad never caught on. He just kept talking. And I walked out of that house thinking, *How did I ever fall for such a douchebag?*

I am not the girl who falls for *that* guy; I can spot the idiot a mile away, and I can decide his intelligence level from the first couple sentences out of his mouth. I use my head; I protect my heart from getting hurt. How was I so oblivious that summer? How did I let him win? But the worst feeling was knowing that even though we weren't even dating, I held Brad to a standard of potential, and therefore I didn't bat an eye at anybody else all summer, whereas I was just another girl Brad will talk about with the guys over some beers when I'm not around.

I am a smart girl, someone you don't mess with. And yet I still fell for the asshole. And what I hate about how this story ended is that I am the kind of person who knows better. I've watched so many people on this earth give too many chances to boyfriends or girlfriends who just treat them like shit, and I've always told myself that that will never be me…and yet I allowed a guy to come in and out of my life whenever he pleased, screwing with my brain and especially my heart every time.

I wish I could tell you that I loved myself too much to give Brad a third chance; but I gave him a third chance. And a fourth chance. However, I still love myself. I still love myself enough to admit that I messed up, and that I will never do it again. I know love isn't perfect, and I don't expect it to be; but I also know that I am happy in my life, and a boyfriend is supposed to be an added bonus to happiness I've already created for myself, not a pain in the ass or someone I feel I have to compete with.

This is the thing about life; we say we're not going to be that person who falls for the douchebag, and yet we probably will at some point be balled up in a corner crying about some asshole who lied to us. That's just the way life is. We like to believe we're ultra mighty, but honestly we're all pretty vulnerable. Vulnerability is why we're all searching for someone special in the first place. But while we're pushing through all those dirt balls trying to find our person, there's something that has to be done in the mean time, and that's falling in love with ourselves.

Life is a process in every single aspect, and I've noticed that when we start to feel like we have it figured out, we are reminded that we still have a lot to learn. I've found that we often are handed things we thought we didn't want, but in the end we realize we needed them all along, whether that's people, opportunities, or setbacks. And through that I've discovered that those damn clichés your parents tell you are always true, like that my sister would end up being my best friend, tattoos are a permanent reminder of a temporary feeling, and that you can't always get what you want (those last two were from my father, coined from Jimmy Buffet and Mick Jagger). There are no promises in life that everything or anything will work out; you could lose your job, you could end up divorced, and you could die tomorrow. There's no say whether you'll ever finish college, find the one, or if you'll be married with kids by age thirty. So while there's so much against each and every one of us in this life, there's only one thing we can learn to do amongst it all to get through: to learn to love ourselves.

Now when I tell you to love yourself, I don't mean to forget everyone else in the world and to become a selfish be-otch. But when everything else is falling apart in the world, you need to know that you always at least have *yourself* by your side. You have to believe in *you*, and you have to trust *you*. We as humans have a neurological need to fill in gaps and have questions answered, so because of that it's crucial to be strong enough within yourself to fill in the gaps when life absolutely sucks. I have to fill in the gaps when I'm falling asleep at night wishing someone was falling asleep next to me. I have to tell myself things are going to work out when five hundred things are wrong in the world and I'm crying.

At the rate my love life is going right now, sometimes I have to only question whether love is really in the cards for me or not. For many people that might sound ridiculous, but I honestly have to do this for myself. Sometimes I fear the idea of love. As I said before, love is a feeling, not a fact, and part of me doesn't ever want to have my head in the clouds. I don't want to lose the things I like about myself, like my work ethic, the responsibilities I have been given, all because my mind is so focused on one person. I don't mean that in a selfish way, but I am scared that I will have to give up part of myself for my person in order to be successful in a relationship. Maybe that is the case with love, and for all I know, maybe that's the beauty of love.

When I look back at high school and all the moments I was sad to be alone, I realize today that it was a good thing I never had a boyfriend growing up, and the same even goes for right now in college. I don't know why, but I have a feeling in my gut that I am supposed to learn about *me* right now; and I don't just mean that in the career aspect. I am supposed to figure out my strengths and weaknesses, highs and lows, what triggers sadness in me, and how I can better myself socially, mentally, and physically. High school showed me what I want in life, and college has been the time to go get it. Every tear I've ever shed since the seventh grade has been partially because I'm frustrated to be my own support system all the time. It's extremely difficult to be your own advice-giver when you see everyone else getting to cuddle up to someone in times of trouble. But through it I've learned what is and isn't worth crying over. I've discovered who will *truly* always be there for me for the rest of my life. I've learned how to stand up to *anyone*. I've explored my own interests, and I've learned what are my passions and what are my hobbies. Because I've never been committed to someone else, I've gotten to know myself a lot better than I think most other people my age get to know themselves. I owe all of that to the opportunities I chased after instead of just chasing after love.

I love myself, and that is a big thing to say. Honestly, how many people can say this about themselves? Of course there are flaws I don't like about myself like my weight and skin blemishes, but at the end of the day, I do not hate myself, and I never have. I consider that a blessing, but I also believe it's because by being single, I've discovered me. I will never stop learning about myself, as the same goes for everyone else; but as of today, I am grateful for everyday of my life so far and the person I've become as of yet. I enjoy being me; not because of my successes, but because I love who I am, and I trust who I'm going to be in this life.

Learning to love yourself before you love someone else is where the heart comes into play when you're figuring out who you are. I have found this to be the most important part of love. When you walk into a job interview, you're supposed to be sure in who you are in order to be qualified for the position. When you're running for a spot on an executive board you're supposed to believe in yourself enough to vote for yourself, with the notion that if you don't vote for you, why should anyone else? These ideas apply just as much to love. Like I said before, I don't believe in following your heart, but I do believe that our heart is what causes our desires in every part of life.

I don't know if love will ever work out for me. As much as I hope it does, I don't sit around waiting for it while I can be learning about myself and helping others. That's not an easy thing to do; I could undoubtedly sit in bed all day frustrated as hell about it if I wanted to. But at this point, I think love is somewhat of a waiting game. Maybe I am supposed to know all these details about myself before someone can love me, but no matter what,

I believe that I have to love myself before anyone else can. I have to be able to say, "I can live with a guy, and I can live without a guy," because if I don't build this type of strength for myself, then there really is no point to get out of bed everyday. If you are unable to realize that there is so much more out there to discover before love, then you are never going to be able to find yourself before you find the one, and *that* is going to lead to heartbreak. I think going after your own goals and forming your own thoughts is what essentially will lead you to the right person in the end; you've just got to fall in love with yourself first before realizing that.

*

As you grow and face the real world, it will become more obvious that you shouldn't major in husbandry but instead grow to love yourself. However, it's easy to think *okay I need to do those things* when you're sitting and doing nothing; it's another when someone disses your outfit or when someone really nice but so not your type asks you out. So to apply this all to real life, proceed to the next page

APPLYING THIS TO THE GAME OF LIFE

Remember, it's a day-to-day process.

It's easy to read a how-to book or hear a motivational speaker and be inspired. It's easy to think *I'm totally going to be a better person and change my outlook on life* after hearing someone else's story of success. It's another to actually go do the crap necessary to live out some cheesy motto you saw last week on a Pinterest board.

When I was in high school I was an active member of the National FFA Organization (Yes, it's that group with the corduroy jackets that was originally known as Future Farmers of America. In the movie *Napoleon Dynamite,* Napoleon and Pedro wore the renowned jacket.). I was by no means a farmer, but the organization did create a strong appreciation for agriculture in me. Every year I went to the state and national FFA conventions, and still to this day for me, there is no sight more beautiful than a stadium full of blue jackets and motivated FFA members. Over the years I have seen countless motivational speakers and retiring FFA officers give incredible, tear-jerking, moving speeches revolving around the idea of leadership. I always left convention feeling revived and like I could do anything…but once I would get back into the daily grind of life that excitement I had at convention with all those FFA members would slowly seep away in the stress of everyday life.

And that's the real enemy when you're trying to make a positive change in your life, or you've decided you're going to spend more time learning you; everyday life. Everyday life is a series of habits we do continuously; it's the opposite of change. It's safe. It's what we know. It's agreeing when everyone around says change is a weird new thing that we're not used to and you should stick to what everyone else is doing. So when we're trying to mix in a new perspective, it often doesn't mix easily with everyday life and occurrences.

I think applying a new thought process to everyday life can be scary in two different ways. For one, it can be just plain hard to make time for yourself. Everyone is really freaking busy these days, and making time for one hour a day to allow yourself for whatever is tough. It's hard to fit the unknown into a tight schedule. However, I think a new thought process is hard when you're trying to move on from something…or someone.

This next part might make me sound crazy, but in my gut I do believe everyone does the same thing, so I'll admit it first. I think as much as we joke about kids having invisible friends, teens and adults also have invisible friends...or invisible significant others. We sure as hell don't usually tell people those things, but I think everyone imagines what it would be like to take a walk in the woods with the person they like, or to order popcorn at the movie theatre with their person. We fill in the gaps as humans; we fill in the gaps of being alone with a pretend love beside us. And this mindset is really hard to break when you're trying to get over someone; it resonates with making a change to your life perspective when you're already against your usual everyday thoughts.

As obvious as it is, change is not an overnight event. To create that excited-about-life-feeling within yourself that you get at a convention, from a good movie, or a vacation, it takes a bit of everyday to find, because it's so detailed it needs time to evolve. Finding you is an everyday process, because it's a switch to your everyday life.

High school feels like forever,
but it's only four years.

...and then you have the rest of your life to live.

I think when we surpass stressful times in our lives; we often forget how stressful those past moments really were. However, I will never forget the hardships of high school.

High school can be hard for anyone; the valedictorian taking A.P. chemistry, the varsity star player who's got their parent breathing down their throat every game, or the in-betweeners who have friends but no specific friend group to feel secure. I was extremely involved in high school with student council, FFA, choir, basketball management, and National Honor Society. I was a Sunday school teacher, and I worked at a movie theatre, of which I was a manager during my senior year. I never had time to relax, and I look back now proud of everything I did, but reluctant that I didn't give myself a second to breathe, because I paid the price for it in anxiety. That time still replays in my head years later when I'm feeling guilty to say no to something in order to give myself a moment of peace, but it was necessary for me to overwork myself to know better than to do it now when I *really* want to succeed.

High school was good and bad, and never easy. There was always a new challenge, whether it was finding balance to get everything done or hoping a guy would notice me. Those four years moved extremely fast, but there were plenty of moments in which I felt it would never end, like once I experienced that feeling of loneliness every student feels at some point. That's what made me feel like an in-betweener; I had friends, I had nice clothes, I was a leader, and I had respect from my peers and teachers, but I still felt like I was on my own (and I experienced that same feeling differently each year). This was a good and bad thing; it kept me motivated to push through to the next day, but in the tough moments it broke me down. Everyone in high school experiences this though; it's not just the in-betweeners or the underdogs. The queen of the cool posse feels it just like the hot senior guy or the dorky freshman feels it.

I'm ranting about this because when you're in high school, you're old enough to be given new responsibilities, but you're also old enough to make mistakes you could pay for the rest of your life. For example you're old enough to get a car, but you're also old enough to get in a car accident that is your fault. You're old enough to get into drugs, and you're old enough to go to jail for it. You're old enough to have sex and you're also old enough to get pregnant. You're old enough to skip school, and never return…which you'll likely regret one day. You are finally allowed to make your own choices, but at the same time you can majorly screw up if you don't somewhat have your shit together. So in the hard moments of everyday life, remind yourself that this phase isn't forever. In less than four years, you can do whatever the hell you want, but right now you've got to get through high school. Even if it sucks, even if you're really not learning anything, you do not want to drop out of this stage of your life. It isn't easy, but there's always someone who can help you through those lonely moments of growing up.

On a lighter note, sometimes it's not the bitches or cool kids, the people who seem better than you, making you feel like a lame ass. Sometimes it's the people you think you're *better* than making you feel like a loser (which in turn is why it's very possible to feel like an in-betweener). Cue prom season.

It's okay to say no.

Everyone at some moment in their lives will be forced to turn a secret admirer down in the love department, and when this dreaded moment occurs, it is the most unexpected turn of events, all the while after allowing everything to make sense and force you to feel stupid for not putting the pieces together earlier.

When I was fourteen, my family and I had just gotten back from church when the phone rang. My dad answered and handed it to me, shaking his head saying he didn't know whom it was.

"Hello?" I answered.

"Stacey?" the person on the other end replied.

"Yes?"

"Hi, this is Carl Shane from church, I'm not sure if you know who I am?"

"Umm, no," I said with confusion of whether or not this was a prank call.

"I'm tall, brown hair?"

He sounded like a fourteen-year-old boy on the phone, but I had no idea who the hell I was talking to.

"No, I don't know," I said starting to give a standoff vibe.

"Oh, well I saw you at church last week, and…I was kind of interested in you," Carl said, ending it as if it was supposed to be a question.

A few seconds passed as I held the phone in shock and agony.

"Umm, I think we should just be friends," I answered annoyed.

"Oh, okay. Well bye then," said Carl.

"Bye."

After I told my parents what had just happened, we looked him up in the church directory, and he was some creepy guy in his mid-twenties! I was *fourteen!* This call made my normal Sunday morning go from nonchalant to a feeling of disgust in my stomach. I eventually figured out who he was in church, and I could just sense him staring at me as he ushered us out of our pew the next couple weeks. Why was someone, who was *way* too old for me, checking me out in church?!

I encountered this same shocking type of incident my second semester of college in my lab class. A girl who lived on my floor was in the same class I was taking for my science credit, and she was sitting next to a guy named Ben. I walked back with them after class one time, and a couple days later when I was walking down some stairs, Ben grabbed my attention with an enthusiastic "Hey!" At first I forgot who he was, but then I recalled our walk back from class together days before. He acted as if we were best buddies, but I didn't mind; when you're a college freshman, you'll take most opportunities available to meet people. We walked to our dorms again together, and by the time it was over I thought, *I made a friend,* which I was rather excited about.

About two weeks later, I ended up sitting next to Ben in class, which was two hours of long ass lecturing following a concert I had been to the night before. I talked to Ben a couple times during those two hours, making jokes here and there, thinking nothing of it.

About fifteen minutes before the last hour ended, Ben said, "So what do you have going on after this?"

Ben is the kind of guy who I could picture getting stuck in the friend zone a lot. He's nice, but he's kind of a Joe-Schmo; not hideous, but not hot as hell, either. He's the guy in high school who would've given anything for a girlfriend but could never get anyone to seriously notice him, and it was occurring all over again for him at that moment.

"I have History of Fashion after this!" I said, completely clueless of his intentions. "I just love that class. We're learning about eighteenth century garments and it's so interesting."

I just went on and on; dumb as a doorknob. Soon class was over, and I was packing up my stuff. I was about to leave, when Ben suddenly said, "Do you want to get dinner together tonight?"

Whoa, I thought; *where the hell did that come from?*

"Umm, sure, yea," I said, thinking that it would be okay to make a new friend and go to dinner with them. "I'm not quite sure yet what I have going on, but I could just text you?"

"Sure!" Ben said.

We walked out of class and exchanged numbers, I all the while feeling completely dumbfounded. I went to History of Fashion feeling so stupid and annoyed. *Great, now I have to kill this boy's dreams. But maybe just going to dinner won't be a big deal? No, I'll lead him on. Fuck me!*

After two hours of contemplating this situation instead of listening to a lecture about eighteenth century dresses, I decided to just break it to Ben when I texted him later that day.

"Hey, I appreciate you asking me to dinner, but it kind of caught me off guard and I'm not really interested in anything right now. I hope we can still be friends and I mean that…you're really cool and I enjoy working with you in class, but I just don't want to lead you on. I totally know how it feels to get a 'no' from someone and I kind of feel like an asshole, but I believe it's just better to be upfront about things."

Ben was probably disappointed, but we were always normal after that; thank God.

Don't get me wrong; the opportunity for me to have a boyfriend has been available. I have been asked out before, I was asked to go to prom by a couple people, and I have been asked to dance; mainly though, by all nerds. That sounds really mean I know, but it's true. It's one of those things I can't deny and be nice about. I was the girl in high school who got asked out only by geeks and squares, and it's probably why I am a bit cold hearted. I often, as in always, run into this issue where either I like a guy and he doesn't like me back, or the guy likes me and I want nothing to do with him. Therefore I have learned that it is indeed okay to turn a guy down if you don't like him.

I have a thing about nerds. I know this chapter may certainly make me sound like an ultimate bitch, but this is my dilemma about weird people: if everyone says you're weird, then there probably is something strange about you that makes people uncomfortable. Especially girls. If guys are the slightest bit weird, girls will run the other direction, no ifs, ands, or buts. I personally have this tendency to hide from anyone who talks to me and has any bit of a quirk to them, because these are always the types of guys who fall head over heels for me. And as I say that, let me remind you that I am well aware of my place in the world; I am a ginger. I know I will never be rated a ten on the sexy people list, and I can't disguise myself for shit. However, I'm that girl who smiles at the nerd once, just once, and is chased down by them for the rest of humanity.

Take Nolan Broka, for example. I was nice to him because he was sitting next to me in art class sophomore year. Thank God he dropped the class, but two weeks before some dreadful seventies themed winter dance, he asked me to go with him as his date. Nolan Broka is that kid who is just not all there and has that horribly eerie voice, and he was the last person I wanted checking me out. So of course, I politely said no to the dance invitation. But did it stop there? Are you kidding me, this is *me* we're discussing. The dance was already weird enough since we had to dress up as disco chicks and hippies, and the moment Nolan laid eyes on me he started following me everywhere I went. I finally had no escape from him in the front lobby, and I was trapped before him.

"Stacey," Nolan called out with his slithering tone, "Wanna dance?"

"No," I said flat out, promptly walking away.

And for the rest of my high school career Nolan creeped me out to a T. I eventually got over my weirdness with him and was able to pleasantly say hi to him when he said hello, but overall I could never get the weirdo to leave me alone. But Nolan Broka is a minimal dose of nerdom compared to Eddie Parthel.

Eddie Parthel was the epitome of a geek. He was this little leprechaun-looking ginger with a high-pitched voice and a whole lot of nerd essence. He had just moved to town, so I was respectful to him since I could imagine transitioning to small town life would be difficult. We said hi to each other the first couple of weeks, however I only meant it in a friendly manner. As I was walking out of a classroom one day, I ran into him. We greeted each other and as I walked away he said, "Hey, I was wondering, would you want to go to the homecoming dance together?"

Shit, I thought. *Why can't I just be nice to someone and not have them fall in love with me?*

"Oh…no, I'm planning to just go with my friends this year, but thanks for asking," I said in the nicest possible way to break someone's heart.

Eddie couldn't hide the disappointment on his face.

It was as if he knew he was going to get turned down before he even got an answer from me and continued to be awkward after that, but we had reached the point after probably a month where we could say hi again. However, I was still majorly creeped out. I didn't want anything to do with him, but it felt like I could never get away from his ass. You know that feeling you get when someone you want nothing to do with is in the same room as you, that feeling of which you almost feel responsible for every weird word or action that comes from that human being just because you know they were interested in you at one point? By the time this happened it was junior year, so between Nolan and Eddie, I had few moments where I wasn't feeling that *hide me, hide me!* fight-or-flight response. Of course nobody wants to get turned down when finally getting the balls to ask someone out on a date, but if it does happen, most people understand that one 'no' means no to any other type of dating occasion, too. However, Eddie did not.

At my high school, prom is decorated and sponsored by the junior class, so once it was my time, prom was all I thought about. I was the leader of my class's prom committee, and being that we were known as the golden class, the class with the go-getters and straight-A students, I wanted this prom to be unforgettable. I also wanted a date for this prom. I knew the odds of me having a date for any other high school dance were very slim, but if I was going to pay damn near four hundred dollars for a dress, there better be a boy escorting me on to the dance floor. Plus, I just wanted to be *that girl* for once. I wanted to be the girl everyone oohed and ahhed at for grand march. I wanted to be the girl who's dress everyone was still talking about on Monday. I wanted to just *look good*, and part of looking good to me was having a date by my side.

Prom was in April, but Valentine's Day is in February, and this happened to also be the time where I was scouting out who I could potentially ask to go to prom with me. I had liked a guy named Seth since sophomore year, and even though he was now a senior and probably not planning to go to prom, I thought that maybe he would go with me anyways. Seth was a great guy; he was super nice, he had an abundant sense of humor, and he was just really relaxed, which I liked. However, I was very unsure whether or not he'd go with me. Seth's one of those guys who are extremely hard to read when it comes to the love department. So in order to not get my heart broken, my friend named Dawn said she would talk to him to feel him out…and Seth wasn't into it. I heard him answering Dawn from across a couple desks in English class one day about what he thought of taking me to prom, and it was one of those instances where he was saying, "I don't know," but in his head he was thinking, *hell no*. So that was a bust. The next guy I considered was Evan. He was someone I was still getting to know, but damn, was he cute. After talking to him more, Dawn gave me the encouragement to text him and see where I could take things. Evan was all into the fact that I worked at a movie theatre, so I thought maybe I could use that to my advantage by inviting him to go to a movie with me. However, he never responded to me when I tried to text him up. That made two prom potentials hit and misses, and God only knew how many more to go.

Then one day when I was sitting in art class, I glanced over to Kristof, the hot German exchange student who had been attending our school all year. And then the light bulb went off. But how was I going to get the attention of this *gorgeous* guy, let alone ask him to freaking prom? I'd hardly talked to him before, but maybe art class was going to be my chance to get to know him. So from then on, I sat next to Dawn and the rest of the seniors, including Kristof, in art class.

A couple days later, it was Valentine's Day. While everyone was getting flowers and chocolates, I carried on with my normal single life, continuously watching friends receive student council Crush sodas and National Honor Society roses from secret admirers. Then art class arrived, and as I molded some disgusting clay together to create some stylish bowl concoction, my friend David walked into the room. With a rose. For me.

"Do you want to know who it's from?" David asked.

I looked at him with much fear, mild anticipation, and an inkling of hope that it would be from a cute, normal guy.

"Nooo," I cringed.

Everyone around the senior table was awaiting the answer.

"It's from Eddie Parthel."

The seniors and myself roared in laughter and

disbelief. Nobody accomplished anything for the rest of the hour. By the last few minutes of class, I sat staring at the rose. *What the hell was Eddie Parthel thinking? And now when am I going to be forced to endure a prom proposal from him? Is there ever going to be hope for me?!* Kristof was watching me as all these thoughts went through my head.

"Dat was pretty funny," he said with his beautiful German accent, "Do you like him?"

"No!" I said with a chuckle, "He asked me to homecoming and I said no, so I'm surprised that he thinks I'd be interested in him."

Well at least this got me to talk to Kristof a bit, I thought. The next day though as I was walking to choir Eddie ran up beside me and asked me to prom. And I, very bitchily I will admit, said no and that he needed to just leave me alone from then on. We never said very much to each other after that.

Nerds are a people group to whom I have no interest interacting with. I know that's bitchy, but whatever. It's really just because I was always the kid who got stuck working with them, and it made me feel like I was never qualified to cross over to the cool group in anything I was doing. To nerds, I am the epitome of that girl we always see in commercials or movies; the girl who the nerd thinks he has a shot with but really he has no chance of getting action from. I really believe this is because I am a ginger; I have one of those nerd characteristics already embedded into my hair follicles that nerds do tribal dances about. But the reality is, I'm not a nerdy ginger, and yes, I do believe I am worthy of more than a nerd for a boyfriend, even though my love life is just as bleak as many nerds' love lives!

This is why I think it's perfectly okay to say no when a guy or girl you have no interest in asks you out. I've learned it's okay to be firm in saying no, and that you don't need to apologize for it. I am a feisty person, and I don't really hide my emotions very well when it comes to these sorts of situations. If you don't like someone, you don't like them. It's not the end of the world, and it's better to just say that right away than to let a guy or girl lust over something that's never going to happen. And for God's sakes, saying no sooner than later is far better than having some weirdo creep on your ass and make you feel awkward for no reason when you're in the same room with them. I've had friends in similar situations before who have said that they feel so bad hurting someone's feelings when they turn them down, but that is the risk a person takes when they ask someone out. It takes serious balls to go up to someone and ask a question that also tells them you're interested in them. I can speak on this, because I have done it. It's extremely nerve racking, but it's the risk we take in order to see if we can make something beautiful happen. You can't be mad if someone says no; you can surely be disappointed, but it's a yes or no question, and neither answer is right or wrong. If you ask someone out and they say yes, great, you've got a hot date; but if they say no, you have to take it like a team player, be upset for a couple days, and move on. You have to look at it as *okay, now I know, and I don't have to think about it anymore.*

I decided I was going to ask Kristof to prom on a Thursday. We had been interacting with each other more and it seemed things were relatively comfortable enough where if I brought it up it wouldn't be too extremely weird. I was a bundle of nerves all day long, and before I knew it, eighth hour art class had approached. Dawn knew I was going to go for it that day, and she was pushing me with every opportunity possible that hour to go ask him. Finally, at the end of class, when people weren't around, I walked up to Kristof.

"Kristof?" I said.

"Yes?" Kristof answered.

"I was wondering; would you be my date to prom?"

"Prom? Hmm," Kristof said, making me die in anticipation, "I don't really know what prom is."

What a fucking dumbass I was; do Germans even *celebrate* prom? A new odd played against me that I had never even prepared for.

"It's like a dance," I said, knowing I sounded like a mix between an absolute idiot and a needy puppy, "people get dressed up, they go to dinner; it's fun."

"Hmm. Okay, I'll go, but only if I get to be prom king," he smiled.

I did it!

"Okay," I laughed, "sounds good, can't wait!"

And I walked back to my locker high-fiving all my friends saying, "I got a date to prom!"

Ironically, that same day my dress was delivered to my house. Everything was working out! My dress fit me perfectly, and I, Stacey Springob, had a date to prom.

This was epic. But I asked Kristof on a Thursday, and he didn't exactly understand what prom was. Sometimes I get this feeling that something I thought worked out isn't going to go through, and then shit hits the fan with it the next day.

And when I was packing up my bag Friday after school, Kristof came up to me and said, "Hey Stacey, about prom...I'm sorry, but I can't go. Dancing is just not my thing, and it has nothing to do with you, it's just not something I'm comfortable with."

We agreed that nothing would be awkward after this conversation and we were still cool, but as he walked away I crumbled in tears. Dawn was sweet enough to come home with me after my dreams were crushed. I started telling her what happened as we got in the car.

There's a specific spot in the school parking lot at my high school that I don't resonate with very well, because when I was having a tough time and needed to breakdown for a second, I always went out to my car at lunchtime and let it all out. And then some stupid sappy song like that "Falling to Pieces" by The Script would play on the radio. It would be like the last five minutes of *Grey's Anatomy* every time. And Dawn, my sister, and I were sitting in that parking lot spot in my car as I went slightly ballistic.

"I'm just so sick of things never working out with guys," I cried, "I liked Seth and that never worked out, and I hardly talk to him anymore. And Evan has no balls; he's just like the rest of those dumb guys. I just want to have *someone*, and I'm so sick of waiting!"

I don't talk to Dawn much anymore, but for about a year and a half she was my best friend. She taught me why people say "I love you" to friends like they say it to family. While I didn't see it at the time, God gave me an amazing friend when I needed one most instead of a boyfriend, and that was one of the best gifts I've ever received.

"You know, everyone has their own issues, and no, Kristof turning you down isn't the biggest problem in the world, but it's important to *you*," Dawn said. "So you've got to look at it as 'okay this is upsetting to me, but I'm going to get through it, and what's meant to be will find a way.'"

I didn't really believe in the whole "what's meant to be will find a way" idea until I met Dawn. While I always knew who she was, we never talked until I was a junior and she was a senior. And all it was that made us become friends was my decision to move over a desk in Media English class next to where she and our other great friend Shannon were sitting. I never would have expected us to become such wonderful friends, I never thought I'd have the balls to ask Kristof to prom, and I never thought I would actually get a date for prom after he turned me down.

After the Kristof fiasco, I was clueless about whether to find another date for prom or not. I was exhausted from my own mind, so I just let it go. But then two days later I was at a basketball tournament and walking into the gym when my good friend Will said, "Hey Stacey."

"Hey Will," I said. I had a lot on my mind at that

moment and really wasn't in the brightest mood.

But a couple seconds later I heard Will say from behind me, "Hey…I was wondering…."

I wasn't sure if he was talking to me still, but as I turned around the back of my brain sarcastically snickered, *would you go to prom with me.*

"Would you want to go to prom with me?" said Will.

I was reliving that moment where someone asks me out and I have no idea it's coming. That star struck feeling overwhelmed my whole system in disbelief and shock; but this time it was a good shock.

"Yeeaaa," I said, starting to become excited. "Thanks for asking!"

And that's when I started understanding Dawn's mantra of 'what's meant to be will find a way.'

I don't know why we fall for people we often likely have no shot at getting. Most days I'm confused as hell and am just trying to make it to the moment where I drop my head on my pillow and can think *I survived today.* Perhaps I was crazy to think I had a chance with Kristof; maybe *I* was the nerd in that scenario. But I think no matter whether you're the nerd who always gets turned down, or the person who is continuously running away from nerds, this whole attack-of-the-nerds in the love department thing is always going to happen, and likely it will happen for people besides me as well. And at least that's because someone on this planet believes in his or her self enough to go for it. I will always give those props to people like Carl, Ben, Nolan, and Eddie, as well as a couple other guys whom I've turned down in the past, because I honestly believe nerdy guys are always the most respectful guys, who would do anything for the girl he's interested in. If a guy, and this goes for any male, likes a girl, he will go after that girl. If a guy wants something, he knows he has to go make it happen; hence why it's so obvious when they like a girl. I believe in saying what you feel, and every time one of my girl friends is crushing on someone, I encourage them to attempt in making it transpire. You never know what could happen.

On a side note though, it is okay for the person who is getting asked on a date or whatever else to say no. They're receiving all this information that so-and-so is interested in them and wants to do something about it, and in about ten seconds they have to make up their mind about it. That *is* a lot of pressure. The whole moment of getting asked out is an art form in and of itself. It's awkward no matter what the outcome. Even though I wasn't always the sweetest in saying no to people like Nolan and Eddie, it is possible to turn someone down politely and still be civil afterwards. All you can do is have an idea of what you would say to someone if you turned them down or accepted their invitation, but you don't have to feel like Satan if you object. You're not committing a crime; it is okay to say no.

As much as everyone rolls their eyes about prom, it still was one of my favorite nights to date. I made prom court, had a great date, and danced the entire night. Prom really did make my whole class become closer. I already felt so loved by everyone after seeing how much they trusted me with making this event come together, but it didn't stop there. I had my victorious moment that night when I was crowned prom queen, and while most people consider this title ultra cliché, it was the cherry on top to an unforgettable night. I never realized how much respect my peers had for me, and for the first time I felt like people noticed me as exactly the kind of person I wanted to be known as. And I must say, it did feel pretty damn good to know Seth, Evan, and Kristof (who by the way went to prom with another girl) saw me in all my glory getting crowned.

Don't say sorry.

While we're on the subject of rejection, don't say you're sorry if you're ending it with someone! *You* have made the decision; *you* are the one who debated this in your head, talked it over with your closest friends to get their consent that you should end it, and *you* have set up the situation to break this person's heart. You aren't *really* sorry about that. It doesn't work with every person you date, and that's okay. I was once advised by my hairstylist to "just date a lot of guys." It's okay to go on a couple dates with someone to feel it out and move on if it doesn't work; it doesn't mean you have to hate each other after that. Just don't say sorry because you want to help the person you're ending it with cope. That's not your job; you're the heartbreaker in this situation, and you just gotta roll with it. When you have an opinion about something, don't apologize for it– that's your fucking opinion, so be firm when you share it with others.

However, you have nothing to lose.

I haven't been on a ton of dates, but I'm always nervous when I'm waiting for the guy to come pick me up. Sometimes it's just natural nerves, and sometimes it's legitimate anxiety. But you have to remember in those squeamish moments that you literally have nothing to lose by giving this person a shot.

I learned this mantra from my friend Dina while studying in California for a semester. She was really good at flirting with guys, and I was quite frankly a dud at it. I never believed in myself enough to think I could actually get a guy to think I'm hot, or cool, or whatever. But Dina would constantly say, "Stacey, you can get a guy. Just go up to him and talk to him. Or get the balls to text him. If it goes bad, WHO. CARES. Literally no one will give a shit if it goes bad, and if it does, you *never* have to talk to him again." Once I heard this I really started thinking about why I'd get so nervous, and I didn't really have a good answer, other than I didn't believe in myself enough when it came to dating. Back then, and sometimes even now, I feel like I can sing in front of a thousand people, I can talk on live television, but I can't talk to a guy. But I am forever grateful to Dina for repeating this to me time and time again, because when you *do* like someone or when a person you *would* be interested in dating asks you out, you have to get over your stupid nerves. You just do. If you never get over being nervous, you're going to be a loner for the rest of your life. When you feel like you're not as whatever enough to score a date with someone, you need to let your brain kick in and listen when it tells you *yes you can*.

Today I always remind myself that people are *human*. It doesn't matter how hot they are or how much more action you think they're getting compared to you, *everyone* gets nervous. I have come to the conclusion when I'm going on a date that I have enough shit to talk about that will impress people. Maybe that sounds cocky, but it's the truth. I've worked on myself, I've spent time doing cool stuff for me, and all you need to show someone on a first date is that you're kind of interesting. And besides, both of you will come prepared with crap in your heads to talk about, because nobody wants to hit the moment of weird silence. It's seriously only awkward if you think it's awkward, so remember the person you're out to dinner with is trying to act semi-cool just like you are, and then get over it! If it goes bad, you never have to go on another date again with that person, but if you are somewhat interested give it a shot. Someone who actually *doesn't* weird you out thinks you're sexy and is interested in you; be excited about that! You literally have *nothing* to lose by giving them a chance.

Guys are so simple, they're complicated.

Why didn't he call me back? What does this text really mean? Did he notice I got bangs? What did he actually mean when he said that? Every girl has asked one or maybe all of these types of stupid questions to themselves regarding some male they're after, myself included. These thoughts in women's heads turn into lunchtime conversations with our girlfriends and spiral into late night slips and over-exaggerations with the guy. That's because girls are nuts. We think everything has a double meaning, we're trying to piece together how the stars align, and we all believe that everything must work out magically, because it always does for the girl in the chick flicks we watch. But here's the thing, and this is something I don't think most girls understand: guys are so simple, that's why they seem complicated. *Girls* are complicated; guys are black and white, night and day. If a guy says "we should hang out," that means we should do something casual with no label, not go to a five-star restaurant and order fillet mignon. If he keeps backing out on you it means he's perhaps scared of commitment. And he likes you in a t-shirt with no make-up on probably more than he does with fake nails and hair done to the nines. That answer you hear in the back of your head, a.k.a. the God-honest truth, when you're trying to figure out those crazy questions running through your mind are most likely the actual answers to what you're wondering about guys. Guys really are yes or no, this or that. If they're picky, they're douche bags, because girls are already picky enough that to have two colliding forces in a relationship would just be too much. Don't overanalyze guys, ladies. You already overly debate everything else in life, so just let your relationship be *simple* and appreciate it for that.

If he likes you, you'll know.

When I was a high school sophomore and crushing on a guy named Seth, I could never decide if he liked me or not. He would flirt with me here and there, but he didn't ever go farther than that. And I, being sixteen and naïve, considered every joke between us, or a hug after a basketball game as a test to determine whether we would eventually be together. Then I remember one night looking at a magazine and reading something that said, "If you're confused about whether or not he likes you, he doesn't." It was a bit of a slap in the face because it was so relative to my situation, but that quote finally made me see that I probably would not be Seth's girlfriend any time soon.

If you're trying to figure out if a guy likes you, you most likely will be able to tell. Sometimes you simply won't see it because you're not feeling the same way (as this is what happened to me when Ben asked me to dinner), but overall, it will be obvious as hell. You will know because he will make sure every time he sees you that he says hi. He will poke at you or try to wrap his arm around you when you're walking or sitting together. He will be willing to share with you, you will notice him looking your way from afar, and he will be the first to compliment you when you accomplish something cool. Guys know what they want and they go after it; it's in their genetic code. There is no debating, there's just what moment should they pick to make it happen. If your feminine radar is telling you that guy has the hots for you, odds are he does. You will know when a guy likes you.

Facebook has changed the game.

We didn't even have Snapchat when I was in high school. Back in my day, if you were caught with your phone you were pretty much shunned from the classroom. One teacher even dropped a fake phone into a fishbowl of water in front of the whole class to get the point across that texting was not welcomed in class. But now the love game is different, because no matter how ridiculous our parents think it is, texting and social media is a part of how our generation connects with people, and it is very much a part of how relationships start. But no matter how technological our lives get, there are some things a smartphone and Facebook will never be able to replace when it comes to love; and yet there's so much they provide that we can't thank them enough for.

Don't text at the damn table.

This whole 'it's okay to text at the dinner table' thing started when I was a sophomore at my homecoming dinner. I was eating at a restaurant with about twenty other kids. We were all decked to the nines, and mind you, twenty kids was one third of my high school class! And yet, people were sitting on their phones the whole night. First of all, my question in a scenario like that one is who the hell do you have to text that isn't already sitting next to you?! Second of all, at any table, a dinner table is for conversation...with the people physically sitting at that table. At my house, phones are not allowed at the table, and I find it sickening when I see a group of people my age at a restaurant all glued to their phones. When you sit down to eat a meal with someone, you are also socially saying you will give your full attention to whoever's at that table and *talk* to them. It's so disrespectful, not that I'm not guilty of it either, when someone is saying something and you are on your phone. Whoever texted you will see that you literally have not read their text yet, and most of the crap people post is the same blessed thing they post every other day. You can wait, at most, two hours to check your phone to instead eat a nice meal and converse with people in front of you. Be the person who doesn't give in to eating dinner with their phone.

Think about how much time you waste on your phone.

If we did the math about how much time we spend staring at our smartphones, I think we would be disgusted. Sometimes I purposely look at what time it is to see how long I have gone without checking my phone, and I'm embarrassed to say it's usually about two to four minutes if the stupid thing is sitting in front of me. That's rancid. I don't have enough fingers and toes to count how many times I've spent a half hour checking all my apps for notifications, and I don't even have that many. So keep that in mind when you're on your phone. Do you really need to check it *again*? You could have just used that half hour you wasted reading a book, going on a run (though I don't blame you for dodging that one), or eating chocolate. If you used all the free moments in a day to do something other than check your phone, you could probably get your homework done before seven o'clock or write a freaking novel. On that note...

Don't be a Candy Crush player.

What I mean by this is don't be like Kim Kardashian ignoring the world with your phone obsession. Ever. And don't admit to being addicted to things like Candy Crush Saga. Don't be that bitch who needs to take a selfie everywhere. People will judge you for those types of things. Your phone is a communication device, but it's not an escape from society…at least it shouldn't be. You still need to know how to make eye contact with human beings and physically speak to them, how to wait in line without a gadget to hide behind, and you should definitely learn how to just *appreciate* a moment. Take one or two pictures if necessary, and move on (I'll admit I'm not a pro at that last part, but I'm working on it).

If you can ask me out over texting, I can dump you the same way.

I am definitely someone who has enough balls to break up with someone in person (if I'm taking the time to end it with someone, I'm going to do it straight up). However, if you asked me out over texting, it doesn't matter how nice you were, I won't feel badly about saying I'm no longer interested the same way. Asking someone out to dinner, breakups, saying "I love you," any big moment like that needs to be done in person; it only gains you more respect from people, especially in a society that is so reliant on sharing tough news through a screen. Back in the day our parents were losers if they broke up with someone over the phone…most kids today are *scared* to talk on the phone. Be brave and show people you know how to use your words in person.

Girls use Facebook like it's the dictionary of humans.

So guys, you know when you're on a first date with a girl and she asks you what you're majoring in and where you're from? She already knows. You know when she asks you about your friends and you kinda laugh because you're thinking about that crazy night out with the boys last weekend? She knows what that weekend entailed. And when we ladies start discussing your family and past girlfriends? We know how many siblings you have and what your ex looks like. And it's all because of Facebook (we just have to ask those questions so there's a verification that you've given us an answer and we get out of looking nuts). We have already scanned every photo down to the pictures your high school girlfriend tagged you in from your senior prom, then we stalked *her* ass and decided she's either a slut or a decent girl, then we see if any of your friends are moderately attractive, we look into that chick who posted something on your wall two weeks ago, and then we make a decision about you. Yeah, kinda fucked up. But that's how it works in girl world. And you won't have any idea it's happening.

I would say the level of Facebook stalking I just explained is the average level (yes, average). Minimal level would be just looking at your pics from an album viewpoint but not viewing them individually, maximum level would be looking through every photo and three months worth of events on your wall (which hardly ever is a lot of useful information), crazy level is if a girl sees every photo, stalks whoever liked it, and checks your profile everyday for new information, and obsessive compulsive level would be everything at the crazy level, plus doing that for every other social media account you have. Every girl has hit maximum level at some point, so consider that a one-time pass, but any girl who does Facebook stalking beyond that should refer back to thinking about how much time you waste on your phone and not becoming a Candy Crush player.

The reason we stalk is obviously because we're nosy as hell, but also because we ladies like to be prepared. Facebook allows us to get some insight into what stupid shit a guy's friends share with him online, if a guy is with the times and even active on social media (Honest to God if a guy I liked didn't have Facebook, I wouldn't date him. Just have a profile to look normal, boy!), and most importantly to see what people are in that guy's life. Facebook helps us understand how many girlfriends you've had, how serious were those girlfriends, how drunk do you get every weekend, and how dorky your friends are. It also allows us to see if you're hardcore liberal or conservative, if you understand a status is one sentence and not a paragraph, and what football team you root for. Then we also like to think that boys will Facebook stalk our profiles, so that's why our cover photos always match the season and we take an insanely ridiculous amount of selfies with our friends...all in the hopes that you might take your freaking thumb and Like it. Yes, we're that crazed about this.

Facebook stalking is where I totally fall short. I love it, I can't get enough of it, and from my experience, I can tell you this Facebook stalking thing isn't going to go away any time soon in the female world of digging up information.

Boys, there's an art to Facebook messaging a girl.

Don't. Ever. Message. A girl. Saying "Thanks for the add". That's so weird! And sure as hell don't ever write that on her Facebook wall. If you want to message a girl on Facebook, figure out something to actually *say*. If you're in class with her, message her complimenting what a great job she did on her presentation today. Keep it casual and invite her and her friends to come out to a party next weekend with your friends. If you like a girl and want to eventually ask her out, have a plan of attack to message her. It doesn't have to be an overthought process, but it just shouldn't be "Thanks for the add" five seconds after she accepts your friend request. That will just equal an ignored message sent.

...and don't over comment.

I'm simply saying this shit to you boys so you look normal. Trust me, and perhaps you've already noticed, girls get extremely creeped out by guys, fast, and Facebook will speed that process up even quicker if you're not careful in how you approach her via the interwebs. If you want to comment on a girl's status or photo, don't ask a question that is completely obvious or just plain dumb. For example, if a girl posts a picture of herself at Starbucks (basic I know), don't comment saying "Nice, what's your favorite Starbucks drink?" That's fucking weird man, especially if you don't know her that well yet. Just Like the photo and look normal. When it comes to Facebook, the goal is to look *not creepy*. Girls like getting a lot of Likes on a picture or status, so your contribution will make her happy; and if she's the least bit interested in you, she will notice that you Liked it, I promise. And then she'll probably start Liking your shit, even if she doesn't really like it. If she starts becoming an avid Liker of your stuff, then it won't be that weird to message her; but DON'T BE WEIRD WHEN YOU MESSAGE HER. Just don't be weird.

Facebook stalking is fun, but as dumb and obvious as it sounds, eventually we all have to come to the realization that we will actually have to *talk* to that person we're virtually creeping on all the time.

Two ways to a woman's heart:
dark jeans and a good cologne.

'Nough said. If you have these two things you already have my attention. Gets me every time.

Every girl dates for marriage.

Trust me on this one. I cannot name one girl I know who has gone into a date with a guy without the notion that if all works out, she's in it for the long haul. Women want commitment, no ifs, ands, or buts. If we only want sex, we will seek out a one-night stand or a friend-with-benefits for that shit. No girl is willing to put her heart into something unless there's a chance it could end with a ring. We have had the ideas of love and marriage ingrained into our minds since we were able to understand who Cinderella was and could play with baby dolls. This is why middle school girls obsess over the guys they're supposedly going out with even though they never actually hang out, and why women have minor panic attacks if a guy doesn't call her three days after the date. When a girl goes on a date with a guy, it's a big deal. All her girlfriends know about the guy she's going to see, and they have all creeped on his Facebook profile. As much as girls say they're this or that, we are often the opposite. We say we're not looking for anything serious, but we will always be awaiting Prince Charming. We might say we don't plan the future out too much, but most girls have decided how great or horrible your last name sounds attached to her first by date two. It's just the way we are. We don't like the unknown, we like to be prepared, and therefore we're not going to half-ass any relationship we're in. It doesn't matter if a girl is sixteen or fifty; she is not dating to just keep dating. She is

Stacey Springob

looking for someone to spend the rest of her life with.

Search for sparks.

I think there are various moments in life for everyone in which some person, quote, piece of art, whatever, informs us that life is short. We learn this simple fact within seconds or over a period of time. For me, this has happened both ways.

The short version might sound extremely cheesy, but I swear there's some substance to it. When I think "life is short" my mind goes to the movie *Friends With Benefits*. Now your sick perverted self might start to think *life is short so we should just fuck our friends*, but that's is not what I'm getting at! It's the scene at the end of the movie with Justin Timberlake and his on-screen dad Richard Jenkins where they're sitting in the airport. Richard Jenkins's character is suffering from Alzheimer's disease and yells out to his long lost love from his days in the military, and it starts a whole conversation that reminds me of the types of things my dad says to me.

"You know, my friends used to say, that when Dee Dee and I looked at each other, it was electric. And I...I let her go. I just let her go. Because I was too damn proud to tell her how I really felt about her. I'll tell you something that I wish I knew when I was your age, and I know you've heard it a million times life is short, but let me tell you something. What this...this...(Jenkins points to his head)...is teaching me, is that life is God damn short and you can't waste a minute of it."

While I feel this quote is powerful on paper, it's the way he says it in the movie that just makes you fear you're wasting your time on something average.

That's my small moment of learning that life is short. My long version was living with my roommate the first semester of my college experience.

When Kathleen and I emailed over the summer we had so much in common. We were in the same major, we liked the same T.V. shows, we had what the other didn't have for supplies in our room; it seemed like we were going to be perfect roommates. But what I found out quickly is that having the same interests really means nothing when you're living with someone you've never met before.

Kathleen has had a rough life, and she was upfront about it from the start. She was born with congenial heart disease, she has had a really traumatic family life, and this was going to be her second try at being a college freshman. Kathleen attended college the year before but only lasted a month and a half. Since I had never dealt with anyone with intense issues like this, I was hopeful and understanding that it was all taken care of during the year she had taken off; however, that was hardly the case.

Kathleen, I kid you not, went to class probably the first two weeks and the last two weeks of the semester we lived together and slept the rest of the time in between. She would sleep *all* day, and it even got to a point where we were on completely different sleep schedules; I would wake up to get ready for class, and she would just be going to bed, and vice versa. She would spend the time she was awake eating Dairy Queen and Kwik Trip fried food from across the street while watching anything from *Friends* to *Seventh Heaven* to Disney movies. She knew when every T.V. show was on, and I finally figured out when I bought my own iPhone that her iPhone was sending her emails non-stop about upcoming T.V. shows. She made me feel crazy in that what I was seeing everyday was a joke, but it wasn't! I would constantly look at her schedule to see if she had class or if maybe I misread it, but I was always right in that she was sleeping during her classes. And what's worse is she would lie to everyone's face about it all when anything was mentioned. Kathleen was obviously in the denial stage of depression, and the past year had apparently done nothing to help her cope with everything back home…and I was the one getting to live with all of it.

I am over the situation, and I am happy that Kathleen decided to stay home the second semester of my freshman year. I truly want her to get better, but what I learned from it all is this: you only live once. Of course that sounds obvious, but I really don't think it is. You only get to go off to college for the first time, leaving everything familiar to you, *once*. You only get to experience the very first semester of college *once*. Of course you can transfer, study abroad, and kind of get that moment back, but it will never be the same. You will never be eighteen again, making your first life transition. I think people, of any age really, don't understand that it's not like you die and get to live again. If you die today, it doesn't matter what you wanted to be in this life of yours; all that's to show is what you were up until your passing. And Kathleen slept her semester away.

I am religious, and I believe God has a plan for me, but I often wonder why God decided to room me with Kathleen. It's not like I wasted my time and needed a message to get moving; I've always been a hard worker with a full schedule. And I don't believe I really taught Kathleen anything, either. She will make an effort every now and then to catch up with some of my friends that were on our floor, but never me (not that I care to keep up with her, either). All I can think is that maybe God wanted the idea that life is short and the you-only-live-once notion to scare me a little, to make me go after whatever it is I really want in this life. That goes for anything in my career or my relationships.

Kathleen essentially made me reevaluate the idea of being average and the fact that most people are completely okay with being mediocre. I don't believe in comfort zones, and I don't spend very much time in them. And it wasn't until Carson came into my life and made me fall head over heels for him that I started feeling the same way about love; therefore, I believe that you should search for sparks when finding love.

Moments are everything to me; it's kind of what I'm entirely chasing in my life. The best moments have sparks; because it's never the seconds of the moment you remember, it's the feeling in the air that makes it memorable. It's when your heart beats out of your chest, or when your stomach drops. It's when you make eye contact and you have to look away to catch your breath. Sparks make me smile like an idiot when I'm walking down the street thinking about that guy or make me nervous when he walks into the room. Relationships should be like *that*.

Searching for sparks is kind of that thing the naïve single girl like me only believes in, you know? In a way, it's still believing in the Cinderella-Prince Charming theory, even though I'm well aware that's pretty unrealistic. However, I do think it's possible to find a strong romantic bond with another person, and to keep it going so there are sparks throughout. Obviously relationships aren't easy, but if both people put in the effort, why can't there be sparks? I try to add some logical explanation with most of my ideas, but searching for sparks is one of those things my heart makes me believe in. I just think if you try to be a good person to everyone, people respond to that, and you're bound to find someone who tries to be the same way if you continue to believe you deserve the best in every aspect of life. That doesn't mean it's going to be easy to get the best, but if you put in the effort, it usually pays off. While it may take till I'm one hundred years old to find *that* guy, that guy I'd choose over Mark Wahlberg, that guy who makes me believe in the beauty of life, I believe *he* is out there waiting to sweep me off my feet. If searching for sparks is cheesy to believe in, then I guess that's the one cheesy thing I support.

Life is all about choice.

This is the thing about life: you *choose* how you live, in every single aspect of it. You choose where you sleep every night, you choose what substances you put into your body, and you choose whom you surround yourself with. Some people would disagree and say that people get stuck because of money situations and what not, but that is not true. You can choose to go into debt now and pay off loans later to have items or an education you dream of. You can also decide to stay where you are and stick to what and whom you have in your life. Either way, *you* decide to stay or go. Often times fear of the unknown, minimal knowledge of other opportunities, or just pure laziness is the driving, underlying force that keeps people in comfort zones. It is a decision to stay in a relationship that you aren't crazy in love with. It's a choice to settle for something less than fantastic. There are factors that seem to be what hold people back from creating a life they really want, but it honestly is our own person, our own mind, that keeps us surrounded by people or places we don't want.

Comfort zones are so easy, especially today with the technology we use to communicate and how we allow people to make relationships casual and not something special. Sometimes life throws us a bone and we keep chewing it because we can. But settling for something less than fantastic is something I will never understand, and this state of mind is what causes disagreements between me and my parents, my sister, and sometimes even my educators. I just don't get why you'd want to be *safe* when you could be amazing.

I refuse to settle for mediocre, because I *know* how to be single. I've done it all my life. So therefore I can be happy with or without someone. I have no reason to just 'hang out and see where things go' with a guy. I am not conceited in this state of mind, but I know what I want, and that is a *relationship*. I have so many other things going on in my life that if I decide to commit to someone, they better be someone who I think is incredible. And really, what's so wrong with believing that you deserve the best? If you're willing to put up with average, then that's what you're going to get, in any aspect of life. You only get this one life to be with someone special so don't waste it on something that's not leaving you feeling anything less than ecstatic everyday. You should be thanking the heavens everyday for the person you're with, no matter what rough patches you're going through. It's a choice to bring or keep people like that in your life.

I thought I'd have a boyfriend by sixteen, then when I didn't everyone told me to wait for college; yet here I am, still single. It is what it is, and I'm actually okay with that. When I watch cinematic love stories or hear some sappy song on the radio, the devil inside me does create a furry of frustration about why I'm still single. But then this overwhelming feeling of an answer comes over me, reminding me that I wouldn't be happy with someone whom I'm not absolutely over the moon about. I've only had a taste of what sparks feel like between a *potential* significant other and me, but it was delicious enough to know that comfort zones are a waste of time and space in this one life we're given. Everyone gets to choose how they want to live, and there's no wrong or right way of doing it. But if you die tomorrow, don't you want to see a life of absolute happiness flash before your eyes, all due to the fact that you waited for the most amazing person to enter your life? Comfort zones are for average people, but believe in your life enough to move beyond that, and chase after the sparks that have, can, and do exist in love.

Decide to *decide* this life is going to be something awesome and worth telling your grandkids about. Allow yourself to welcome in the idea that something could be better than it is right now, especially with your relationships. Make an effort to reach out to old best friends to catch up over coffee, or to save a couple dollars so you can send Christmas cards out this year. Tell yourself you *can* go on a date with that person and it *will* be fun and not awkward because they're just as human as you are, and they will be just as nervous and prepared with stuff to talk about like you will be. You are allowed to have a fabulous life, filled with loving people who only bring you up…allow yourself to believe you can find it.

Know your limits.

I don't have tons of crazy college stories, but one story that does come to mind is something I never thought I would actually encounter when I was living in the dorms. One Saturday night at around twelve thirty I decided to turn in early. I climbed into my lofted bed, tucked myself into my blankets and closed my eyes, ready for a good night's sleep; and suddenly I heard some moaning through the wall coming from the next room over. It was sex moans! I cringed under my blanket more and more as it got louder with each scream. I couldn't believe what I was hearing, and it made me feel like a complete loser. I've run into people making out when trying to clean out movie auditoriums back home at work, but I never thought I would have to encounter *this!* I can officially say that nothing makes you feel more stupid about your lame love life than hearing sex moans coming from the room next door. It's just a reminder of all the action you're *not* getting.

Holding hands. Cuddling. Fooling around. Sex. Let's be real– these are half the reasons we look forward to being in a relationship, and we very well should. But in today's world filled with sluts, manwhores, emotionally distressed individuals, sex-filled media, and the idea of making sex seem so casual, there is one thing that needs to be made clear; sex is not casual by any means. It can really do some damage to a relationship, between friends, or to your own self esteem, and that's why it's so important to know your limits with sex, and really anything having to do with "touching" (I know that word sounds so creepy, but there's no other way to put it!).

I have a confession to make; I used to have what I call a "touching" phobia. It started at around age sixteen, one of the roughest years of my life. I was having a tough time with classes, I still hadn't found my niche in high school, and I was just very unhappy. I remember noticing how so many people hugged each other during the school days, and it kind of bugged me. *Why do people feel a need to hug each other all the time*, I would think. My gloominess started making me feel secluded from a lot of people, especially with any form of affection. While I believe everyone has some type of "bubble," my bubble was *extremely* fragile, and if anyone was two inches too close to me I couldn't handle it. The idea of dancing with someone at prom, hugging anybody, cuddling, just being affectionate with touch, freaked me out. And everyone knew about this touch-o-phobia of mine; still to this day I have people I know from high school who look at me twice before going in for a hug. I've really never been crazy affectionate, but for about four years I wanted *nothing* to do with affection.

This touching phobia has really impacted my life with guys I've been interested in. Here's the thing: when I like a guy, the idea of being cuddly and loving doesn't scare me. However, if a guy is more interested in me, I feel *super* anxious and stressed, almost to an unhealthy level. This happened nonstop with Sean. Sean and I talked a lot when he was off at college, but I never allowed us to hang out through our year of texting before I went to school partially because it caused me major anxiety. I was not ready to hold hands, cuddle, kiss, nothing. It had nothing to do with the fact that he had been in relationships before, or that I didn't trust him; I just was not ready for it all. I was lucky that Sean was a nice guy and waited for me to get over my touching issues. Eventually, when I was ready, he was my first kiss. It wasn't filled with fireworks or like we see it in the movies, but it was safe, and exactly what I needed to realize I can be affectionate and survive. And I am proud to say I am a survivor! I no longer have a touching phobia (one will get over a phobia like this pretty quickly after starting college and living in such close quarters with people!).

Though you probably think I'm officially crazy learning about my touching issues, my problems taught me something important, and it's that you need to know your limits with sex and anything having to do with touching and affection. For some people this might sound crazy; but there are so many reasons in this day and age to know what you are and aren't comfortable with doing.

Let's be real here; I don't know anyone who got a decent education about sex and relationships in high school compared to how much we were told we shouldn't smoke cigarettes and weed every school year. It's a weird topic for teachers and parents to discuss with teens and young adults; however, if you've ever turned on a T.V., listened to the radio, if you've ever opened an issue of *Seventeen* or *Glamour* magazines, you know what sex is. And despite what someone's religious beliefs or lack thereof are, sex is something a person can act on, even at a ridiculously young age. So it really does need to be discussed, but in health class all you learn about is how sex works in order to create a human being. You're told what happens, and how to prevent it with condoms or birth control. But let's be honest; that part isn't what we analyze when we think about having sex for the first time! We're thinking about how self conscious we are, if we'll disappoint our partner, if it's feeling how it's supposed to and so on. The experience and the emotional side of sex wasn't mentioned once in my health class, because that's the part that's weird to discuss between adults and teens. It doesn't matter your gender or sexual orientation when it comes to this topic; everyone is going to go through the same thoughts and anxieties with sex. Sex isn't just baby making (We are in the twenty first century!). Despite what your pastor or religious aunt tells you, sex is something special between you and another person, no matter if it's before or after marriage. It's supposed to be special; when the experience disappoints someone it's because we expected to feel happy afterwards.

So let's talk about what they *don't* talk about in health class...sex is showing someone your most vulnerable self. There's really nothing else to it. It doesn't matter if you have sex with one person your entire life or one hundred; sex is showing someone *you*. Some people take this to heart and only have sex with a few people throughout their entire lives, others have lots of partners because they use sex to fill a void. So when you're in high school and you're old enough to have sex but also old enough to deal with the consequences, it is not just getting pregnant or an STD you have to consider. You also have to think if you'd be happy with yourself, with this choice you've made to show someone a side of yourself that quite honestly I'm not sure many people completely *do* know during their teenage years.

My faith definitely plays a big role in my love life, as I know it does for my friends who are religious, too. However, I didn't start thinking about my limits until I was about fifteen. When I was a freshman in high school, a man named Chris Stefanick came to our school to talk about sex and dating, and he taught me that it is crucial to know your values and limits regarding your sex life *now*. That may sound strange; why would someone care about how they feel towards having sex with someone if they weren't in a relationship, and at that time, why should I have cared about my limits with sex at age fifteen? Well think about it; if you don't know *now*, how likely are you to make a decision you're truly comfortable with in the moment with someone when things are getting hot and heavy? The last feeling most people ever want to experience is regret the next day after fooling around with someone when they weren't actually ready to.

You will meet people with all different ideas regarding sex. I have friends who have had sex with twenty different people, and I have friends who are waiting till marriage. In today's society sex is plastered all over media, it's what you joke about with your friends and hear the upperclassmen talking about, and it's not a big deal to have a one-night stand on Saturday night. But no matter what you believe, *it is a big deal*. How you feel the next day about the choice you made matters. What you consider an invasion of privacy or respect matters.

It's not just God, if that's what you believe, who makes you feel a sense of emotion towards your actions in your sex life; it's your conscience, and everyone has one of those, some more than others.

I also believe that by knowing your limits with sex, you are labeling the level of importance for your future; meaning, by deciding to have sex, you are also answering that you would be okay with the consequences if it backfires on your ass. I always think if you are ready to have sex then you are ready to be a parent, because pregnancy is obviously a risk in making this decision to go all the way. And if you do decide to have sex and you don't use some type of protection, it is only a matter of time before you get pregnant. There are no "risks" with this type of thing; it *will* happen at some point. By the time I turned twenty years old, I knew seven teen moms. Don't be stupid. Wrap it up.

Lastly, another major reason to consider your limits with sex is a little something called an STD (sexually transmitted disease). This doesn't sound like anything major usually until you get to college. Is it *really* worth having sex with someone you met at a frat party but have never talked to before that in your life? This is the type of thing you risk happening if you aren't careful. It only takes once to mess up the downtown for the rest of your life. I think it's safe to say whatever your values are with sex, there is kinky and there is just plain stupid. One night of steaminess shouldn't come back to haunt you for the rest of your life.

Once you have decided your limits, I also believe you

should be willing to admit to your actions if you decide you are ready for sex. Even if you're not having sex, but you're fooling around with someone, you have to be willing to own up to it. If you are getting funky with someone and people are even a tiny bit aware, you have to be willing to admit to it if you get asked about it, fair and square. I feel you'll get more respect for just being honest than denying it. Most people just want to know and then will move on.

And if you are discussing sex with a potential partner, you have to be honest about how many people you've had sex with, if you've never had sex, whether or not you're on birth control, or if you have an STD. How disrespectful would it be to lie about something like that? Anyone and everyone has a right to say they're not ready to have sex or that you've had sex with too many people for them to risk getting someone else's leftover cooties. And it also goes the other way around; if you're a virgin, say so, but be smart enough to know that people can walk all over you with that kind of information. You don't want to fall for someone who is just waiting to get in your pants and then drop you right after.

Somehow I got on this topic with a friend at college named Cameron. She told me how she dated a guy named Jonny for three years in high school, and they had sex one time when they were seniors. However, they broke up pretty quickly after. Cameron said it was her first time having sex, but it wasn't for Jonny. And that one time still affects Cameron to this day. She said she sees Jonny when all their friends are together, and while she's cool with Jonny, he still has this part of her that she can't ever get back. I wish words on paper could grasp the annoyance and frustration Cameron had about this, still, *years* after their break-up. Cameron said it doesn't matter how much time has passed or that she's moved on; she gave Jonny all her vulnerability that one time, only to later watch Jonny still triumphantly have the memory of that one night as a medal of prestige today. And this conversation gave me a new perspective on evaluating how far a person decides to go with another individual.

Having said all this, know that I love guys. I love how they're this or that, to-the-point, how they can be silent amongst one another and content at the same time, I secretly love their dirty jokes and remarks, I love when they walk past and I can smell their cologne a second later, and I miss their ability to not take life so seriously when I've been around girls for a while. But amongst all that, I must say, guys really do talk with their penis. You know how they say "The penis does the picking?" It really does. I mean I genuinely do believe that guys value characteristics like brains and humor as much as girls do, but let's be real; the minute a girl brings up even the *potential* of any sexual activity to a guy, he's *all* ears. Girls have a lot more at stake than guys do with casual sex like pregnancy and STD's, and I think that's why we tend to assess it more. Not to mention the fact that girls overanalyze everything; think about how much a girl can analyze the meaning of a single text message. Now times that by one thousand and you've calculated how much they will analyze one afternoon delight. And this is why

Cameron still regrets giving her virginity to Jonny. To him it was having sex again, but to Cameron it honestly was giving away a part of her to someone she thought she could trust. Guys don't always consider those aspects of having sex. It doesn't make them demons, but it can really screw with girls' heads if boys are talking themselves up with their dick and not their brain.

I think when it comes to things like sex it is completely okay to be selfish, because even though it takes two to tango, sex is just as much about the individual as it is the experience between two people. Sometimes people are just really horny and need a fast break. But everyone knows that we only end up learning the hard way if we rush into something we're not ready for. There's a reason sex makes everything complicated, and it's because people don't think about their limits and what they are or aren't comfortable with. It doesn't matter whether you're religious or not, you have to know how far you're willing to go *now*, because the consequences could potentially change your entire life if you aren't careful, but it could also be something tough to deal with emotionally if you do it before you're really trusting in the other person. Even if you don't completely know what your limits are, just having an idea of things like whether you're going to wait for marriage or not is important enough to start with. Are you okay being friends-with-benefits with someone, or do you want to be in a relationship? How long do you have to know someone before you'll drop your panties for them? It sounds obvious, but if it were so obvious we wouldn't have so many teen pregnancies or college students with STDs. Respect yourself enough to know how long you want to wait, if you want to wait at all, and who is it you're waiting for (yourself or God, for example). It doesn't matter whether you're a virgin or not; maybe you have had sex before and you've realized you're not ready for that phase of a relationship yet. Then slow it down. Just because you've already had "your first time" doesn't mean that you have to keep a pattern you don't like continuing. Your decision about your sex life isn't your parents', your friends', or your partner's decision; it's your and only your decision, and you should love yourself enough before you love anyone else to know that. So ask yourself, what are your limits with sex?

Make your religious beliefs a non-negotiable.

As I discussed earlier, once you've figured out yourself, it will be easier to figure out what you want in a person you're dating. As I say this though, knowing my friends and myself, you should not bank on your religious beliefs if you have them.

If you're in a relationship and you haven't discussed your religious beliefs or lack thereof, then you better get on that pronto, because religion for faithful people can be a deal-breaker. Most people who are faithful to some religion or belief system hope to find someone who practices something within the same vicinity. My mom, my sister, and I are Lutheran, but my dad is Catholic. It's something that a lot of people find peculiar, but Lutheran faith and Catholicism are relatively similar. There are differences, but the biggest differences only make for good debates at the dinner table. Our differences in religion work for our family, but that might not always be the case for everyone else. If you are solemnly set on marrying someone who practices what you personally believe in, then that's something you've got to make a priority. One of my best friends is Mormon, and she only dates people who are Mormon as well. She plans to continue making her faith a main aspect of her life, and so it is crucial that she finds someone who supports that with her. It really doesn't matter what age you are; you could be thirteen or sixty, but if you practice a religion and truly value it in your life, then make that a non-negotiable personality trait to find in someone else. You don't want to discuss religious differences after you've already signed marriage papers or you're deciding whether or not to baptize your kid, so make it important now; it'll only help you find someone who fits your personality that much better.

Half of life is showing up.

This might be kind of random, I don't know, but it is

something I really have come to discover from being single. I've been discussing how life really is all about the people in it, and in order for you to keep connections and relationships with anyone continuing, you have to make an effort.

I think when you're single you definitely have to do more work to keep up with friends, because you have no link of mutual friends to help you do the work like you do in a relationship. That involves texting someone when you know you're both on a holiday break and asking to catch up for an hour or two. It's being that person who gets all your high school or old college buddies together when everyone's in town, or driving across the state or even country to see your best friend once a year. It's as simple as a happy birthday Snapchat and could be as big as one day standing up in your friend's wedding. In the moment, it is extremely easy to say you'll hang out next time with that person or to bail on a party, but it is more important than you think to make an effort and reach out to people you care about. I have no problem admitting that there are days (actually a lot of days) where I don't want to talk to anyone, but I know I will regret it later on in life if I don't continue friendships I've built with people over the years. I know adults who kept in contact with people from their past and adults who didn't, and the adults who didn't have very few close friends today.

I didn't realize how important this idea of "showing up" was until I got to college. When I was in high school, I always attended dances, basketball games, and whatever else to support friends even if I didn't want to necessarily go, because that's just what we were taught growing up. We're supposed to support one another. The same went for academics; even if I hated a class, I didn't skip it just because it was hard. I showed up and gave it my best effort. So when I got to college, I expected everyone to have this mantra, especially since college is something people *choose* to attend. However, I discovered not everyone understands the value of showing up, and this can kind of play to your advantage in college. The professors trust the kids who don't skip, and the upperclassmen leaders believe in the youngsters who attend every meeting for extra curricular activities. If there is any one way to score brownie points with people in life, attend the stupid meeting, pick up the work shift, or go to the party for an hour. People notice the people who make an effort.

Think about it; if that guy or girl you like sees you showing up to events, they can tell you're dependable, and that likely will help you get their attention. The reason I said earlier that I do think Carson notices me is because there's been things he's mentioned in the past when we're catching up about who I was in high school that I never in a million years thought he ever noticed. And for a girl to know that a guy noticed her is a BIG deal, even if it was back in the day. People want trust in relationships; we want someone we know will listen to how great or horrible our day was. That person who will listen isn't the person who comes in and out of our lives (even though we sometimes hope it will be– a.k.a. how I hoped Brad would be); it's the one who always is there for us, no matter if we're crying tears of joy or ugly face crying. If you show up in life, the world will reward you for it. While it doesn't always feel like it, people notice the people who make an effort to stick around.

If you can talk about poop with someone, keep them around.

Yes, you read that right.

I am a firm believer in this and it has been proven to me time and time again. If you can bring up the subject of poop with someone, and you know that only is a subject that will go into more detail, that person is worth keeping in your life. I'm not talking just dog crap here, I'm talking real human feces. If you can discuss this with someone and they don't flinch once, that's a great sign. Think of all the people you've had a legitimate conversation about poop with…they're always the coolest people in your life! But poop conversations don't just tell you who's the shit and who's not (See what I did there?). Poop can tell you what kind of person someone is. If you're talking about this subject matter and someone can only say the word 'poop', then they're probably someone you don't want to swear too much in front of, a type-A sort. If someone says 'crap', they likely have a decent balance of both book smarts and street cred. But if someone says 'shit'– you know they're fun. And the more enunciation on the word, like when they use the back of their throat and say SHIIITT, that'll indicate they are *really* fun. I never thought I'd say this, but poop can open doors; it can help decipher how comfortable you can be around a person, because it really is something not everyone feels content to discuss. I'm not necessarily saying test this experiment out by bringing it up at the dinner table, but if poop, crap, or shit is mentioned in a conversation and no one flinches, all systems go!

Projects aren't people.

I have realized now that I'm in my twenties that there is a difference in the way you view and want relationships as you grow up. When I was sixteen, and again when I was eighteen, my thought process was I want five hundred different things right now, and a relationship would be nice to squeeze in, too. Now I want two or three things, and a boyfriend is one of those.

But as I get older, I realize the need to feel loved, the want to love and have it returned in movie night cuddles, dates, Instagram pictures— it doesn't matter whether you're taken or single— love affects EVERYTHING. It affects *everything*. Love makes certain people outgoing so someone will notice them, it makes some people work extra hard to show off their talents to impress people that way, it keeps us up at night, it's taught us how to be great Facebook stalkers; love has a say in everything we do.

And what I've learned from my success in school, work, travel, is that projects aren't people. Projects end, deadlines are met, but people are always there for you, and you always want people. You know you're always anticipating a last day with a project or a job, but you don't usually associate that with people.

The end of my story with Brad made me start thinking about this. Things didn't really end pretty with Brad; we were basically fighting through texting about the same shit we had been for two years already. But at the end Brad said, "A relationship isn't a business," referring to the fact that this is how I tend to think in terms of everything. It wasn't really a shock that Brad said this to me, but I do keep it in the back of my mind, because he was right. I will fully admit that I have a hard time separating work from play, especially since my interests kind of overlap in creativity. This *book* overlaps work and play for crying out loud. But while my book discussing what I've learned from never having a boyfriend intertwines two different parts of my life, it still is a different component to whom I will be when I *am* in a relationship. What I've said here will obviously be applied to my life then, but that will be a different phase and there will be things I will learn from actually *having* a boyfriend that I can't learn from being single.

I love the movie *Silver Linings Playbook*, and there's this line in the movie where the lead actors say, "read the signs". Throughout the movie they keep asking, "Are you reading the signs? Are you reading the signs?" And I find as I keep growing that that's what you have do in life.

You've got to read the signs. The signs of the universe are so clear, but we screw it all up with our emotions, and we make it complicated with our feelings.

The signs in my life have told me for a very long time that I'm going to be successful in my life. And today, that is more evident than ever. I know that sounds conceded, but it. is. clear. I have the drive to go the extra mile, to take risks, and I will keep doing that. And that drive, that passion, to *really* go after what I want, is something about ninety percent of this world doesn't have. I've seen it time and time again, and you will see it if you push yourself to go after leadership positions, to finish high school, or to go on and finish college. I *am* going to be successful. It is the signs of the universe telling me that. I'd be stupid not to follow those signs. But love and relationships always make me wonder if I'd be happy taking a detour.

Wanting to be in a relationship is not the biggest problem in the world; there are obviously more important matters. But when I think back to being sixteen and crying in my car in the parking lot about just wanting to be with someone, feeling that hole in my gut…to now be in my twenties and *still* crying about that same thing once in a while…it makes a person kind of question the signs. It makes me think *you've got to just keep going, you're meant for the big career, you gotta do it,* but then I realize careers don't save you. Careers keep you occupied. Projects, our involvement with activities, they keep us busy, but they aren't people. And that is what I struggle with the most. When the deadline is met, the project is done, but people don't end. A relationship, a good one, *lasts*.

I can see where people have a hard time reading the signs. Because life is all about this balancing act; you have to balance people and you also have to balance projects. You can't be around people too much, because you need to invent yourself, but at the same time you need support. You need support but getting too much of it can make you overly dependent on people...do you see where we might get stuck? We either rely on people too much for balance or we rely on work to keep us occupied. That's why we have girls who major in husbandry. That's why we have guys who only go so far with dating and say "whoa too much, I can't commit". And that's why we have workaholics like me.

I think we're quick to point out the people who use people to fill voids in their lives, but we don't always point out the people who do the same thing with work. We all have a friend with that dad who works *all* day, then is too tired to enjoy the family when he gets home. We all know the girl who lived for getting straight A's in high school (I'm most definitely sure I was that girl according to some of my classmates). However, if you work yourself too hard, that's all you're going to know, and you'll realize projects aren't people when it's too late. I struggle with this, but I know you can't look at your relationship with your person the way you do work. They are two entirely different things. You can't schedule your life with marriage and babies the way you can schedule project deadlines, because that's just not how life works. I do believe what's meant to be will find a way, but at the same time you can't ignore love just because you're busy working. It's not worth it to plan every aspect of your life, because newsflash: it's not going to go according to plan! Ever! Sometimes I'll meet people who immediately resonate with me because we have the same drive to be successful, but I also meet people who have that drive and don't know anything else. I could have easily become that girl, and to some people I probably *am* considered that person, but I've learned you really need to step back and smell the roses a guy left on your doorstep here and there.

Even though in our minds the future has a certain picture to it, sometimes the signs of the universe in this present moment have a detour for us to take. It doesn't mean you can't get to where you want to be, but projects aren't people. You can't plan out how people are going to come in and out of your life; you have to enjoy who's along for the ride *now*. And if that scares you, guess what; it will scare you no matter what. It's life. It's happening as you read this. And you don't get a lot of it so you have to learn that while your job is great, it's eight hours a day, forty hours a week, and the rest of life is about the people in yours.

At some point in your life, you're not going to want five hundred things plus a relationship; you're literally going to ask the heavens for two or three things, with one of those being the person you love. So if you can learn now how to balance what you love doing with the people you plan to keep around, you'll learn how to have a plan while taking life as it comes, and you won't need to fill any void with work or people.

You choose to be in a relationship.

I think getting into a relationship is kind of like signing a contract before you start a job. You've only seen the positive aspects of this potential partner, but for all you know you could be dragging yourself into a pile of garbage. You're saying yes to something of which you have no idea whether or not you'll really like it. No, you're not signing a contract for marriage, but you are saying you're going to commit to this person you care about; especially if it's a long distance relationship. I give people in long distance relationships major props. Whether it's military girlfriends or college graduates taking on their first jobs, long distance has to be a bitch. However, nobody forces you into a relationship, and that's why I believe you have to take responsibility for your fights, hardships, and challenges you face in one. You have to figure out a way to make it work.

We all try to look for people who are somewhat similar to our quirks and passions; therefore, we hope they will also have our same values. If you share equivalent values with your partner then you should find a way that works for both in getting through the days that make you think you're crazy for signing this contract. It's okay to vent every now and then to your girlfriends or your boys about what's troubling you in your relationship, but I'll be honest; any single person who's wishing they weren't doesn't want to listen to your complaining all the time. *You* decided this is what you wanted. While there might be rough moments, you still have someone texting you, calling you babe, and a person to listen to your midnight rants. Single girls get *Eat Pray Love* and chocolate for that shit.

I'm not telling you this stuff to make you feel bad that you're in a relationship. I'm telling you this so you appreciate the fact that you are. You've been blessed to find someone who's willing to give a damn about you and your problems. Never take that for granted, even when there are fights. Those little things that drive you nuts about your relationship are the barriers you have to conquer together (it's in the fine print of the contract). When someone asks you to be in a relationship with them, they're also saying "Will you stay with me through the good, the bad, and the ugly?" You agreed that you would say, "Yes."

I do agree that yes, when you're single you mainly worry about yourself; but I think that's the reason we all want to meet our person. Girls need someone to basically tell our minds to shut up when we're overanalyzing things, and guys need someone to tell them to wake up and get their shit together, to put it bluntly. I think we all drive ourselves a little crazy, and let's face it; it's wonderful to have someone else's interests become something you suddenly value, even when it's something you had absolutely no care for before you knew the person. We love finding someone special because it opens up a whole new world of insight to us. That's the beauty of love. We find someone in the hopes that they'll make us a better person. As much as I enjoy meeting new people at college, joining different groups with the means to grow as a human being, I get tired of always having to make *myself* grow. I want to support a guy in his interests and get the same back. I want to be opened up and welcomed into someone else's world. It's nice having free time to sit and watch the *Keeping Up with the Kardashians* until you can't watch another minute, but it would be fun to watch a Packer game with a boy, too.

So if you find yourself in a relationship that causes you frustration, I have this to say to you: you chose to be in this relationship. You signed your name on the dotted line of the contract even though you knew it wouldn't always be easy. That doesn't mean you can't vent about issues every now and then, but it doesn't necessarily mean you can complain, either. It does mean, though, that you believed in the value of having this person in your life enough that you agreed you'd be willing to work it out when the tide rolls in. Appreciate everything, and be thankful even if you aren't meant to be together forever that this person was brought into your life and opened you up to a new view of ideas and opportunities.

The longer you wait, the more you'll value what's to come.

My sister Amanda is entering the age where a boyfriend is entirely what fills the space between all her other ideas and thoughts, and as a big sister it terrifies me. She is however, for the most part in the same boat that I was at her age; single and really hoping for someone special. We discuss boys and the adventure of falling in love a lot, and I'm thankful that she also notices the choices and consequences of people around her like I do. One day we were in the living room watching T.V. and discussing those high school girls who always have a boyfriend, and this girl Sara came up in particular during our conversation.

"Sara's brother said she's had like eight boyfriends already," Amanda told me, "You know what I just don't get about people like that? At that point, when you're not even eighteen years old yet, how can anybody really worth your time become truly special after having that many relationships already?"

I was shocked and yet so proud that my sister realized this valuable aspect of love at sixteen years old, because just knowing that alone will save her so much ridiculousness in the love department. And with that, I must point out that when you're still anticipating your first relationship with someone, the value you put into what that first relationship will be is everything, and definitely incomparable to a girl like Sara (no offense, Sara). The idea alone of who my first boyfriend will be means ten times more to me now than it did when I was sixteen, and it even meant a lot to me then. That said, I think any aspect of love, whether it's a relationship, sex, whatever, will have more meaning the longer you wait. The longer you watch other people rush into things, the more you'll realize not to do the same, and you'll start to really understand that good things take time to come together.

*

So here you are. You've made the decision that you are going to start learning more about you; even though you know it's not that simple because you still have to go to school with people who drive you nuts or work with losers. Just remember that it's a day-to-day process. You learn a little bit about who you are gradually, and while some things like high school and even college can feel like forever, it's (usually) four years, and then you have the rest of your life. You might be the pretty girl who gets a lot of attention, you might be the hot guy all the girls swoon over, or you might just be an in-betweener. But that's perfectly okay. You'll figure out as you learn about yourself why you are in the supposed hierarchy of popularity you are in (and it could be for a reason you love or hate). Know that it's okay to turn someone down if you don't want to date them, but that someone can do that just as quickly to you. However, if they don't creep you out, consider giving that person a chance if you have nothing to lose by saying yes. You are entirely worthy of finding someone who makes each day a little better with just their presence, so belief in yourself, your life, and search for sparks. Life is all about choice, so decide you're not going to be a creep on social media, but remember to keep those around who are cool enough to handle the discussion of poop. Decide what you are and aren't ready for in the bedroom now, so you don't regret it later. Remember in the little moments that half of life is showing up and projects aren't people. And don't complain about your relationship too much, because you chose to be in it (and single people don't wanna hear it).

Making the mental note that you're going to start devoting time to figuring out yourself is fantastic, but then you have to actually do just that. Let's be real; there's always going to be some challenge, person, or shortage of time that makes you feel like you can't or don't deserve to study your interests and invest in them to create your big picture. But if you continue to tell yourself it will be worth it in the end (because it will be), you will get there. The doubters and the obstacles you face now won't be around forever. Creating your big picture is easier said than done, but it's also completely necessary to find balance between work, play, the brain, and the heart.

WHEN YOU'RE AT THE BIG PICTURE

There will come a time when you are applying all this crap I've discussed to your life, and in the midst of finding yourself, you will realize you've done just that.   And before you start doing the work of soul searching, of separating your heart from your brain, you will imagine this moment as your wedding day, the day you graduate college, or the day you become a parent. But it probably won't be any of those days; most likely it'll be the days when you're just sitting in your room thinking about life and how you've evolved over time, in the middle of reading a good book or listening to an interview of someone you admire. It'll be on a car ride going home or the last days of being far away from everyone you know. When you realize you've reached the place you need to be at for your big picture, you'll find it in a moment that is *not* about someone else, because that's where a good relationship starts; with you. The little moments are what create the big picture, and you'll be looking back when you realize you've found it.

So once you've found your big picture, once you've reached what you consider the top, you'll find life is not really about the big picture. Even though that's what we base it on, it's one component, but it's not everyday. But it still is important to have a big picture; it's what ignites us to do something with our lives; to move to a big city, go after our dream job, to get the balls to ask someone out, to say, "I love you". The big picture is an idea of what we consider perfection, and quite frankly the big picture can change and likely will evolve throughout your life. We always have new goals, but one thing's certain; we tend to take the same people through it all with us who have been there from the day we decided we needed to figure out ourselves before figuring out anyone else. So as we're going through life, adding and nixing things from our big picture, we can't forget about the people who are always there during the little moments– the moments that will one day be remembered better than the big picture itself.

If they don't make you a better person, leave them.

It was almost 2 A.M. and freshly New Year's Day 2012. I was still at work finishing up yearly inventory with my co-workers Lori and Jaden. I worked at a movie theater while in high school, and throughout my senior year I was a manager. On that shift I had been at work for almost twelve hours, and I was stressed that I messed up calculating the right numbers for napkins and Wildberry Skittles, along with dreading my soon-to-be vicious drive home through an incoming snowstorm. What a way to bring in the New Year, huh?

I learned a lot from being a manager my senior year of high school, but it also is why I get frustrated easily. It was hard for my friends to understand the anger I constantly carried around at that time in my life. I often went from eight hours of being a high school student straight to eight or nine hours right after as a manager, in charge of a building and taking a deposit to the bank at midnight. That's a responsibility most of my friends couldn't grasp at that age, not that I blame them. But it made it hard to relate to my peers after a while, and this carried into my freshman year of college. The reason everyone anticipates a student's freshman year of college is because the student is suddenly forced to problem solve every situation they're handed; but I had already learned problem solving on a completely different platform by that point. Rather than figuring out how to problem solve for myself as a college freshman, I learned how to problem solve as a high school senior for a business, and that meant every gamble I took not only impacted me, but potentially lots of other people. This kind of pressure created a stress in me that could make me freak out over practically nothing at the time, and my friends didn't know how to react to it. So rather than freaking out at people, I held the stress in.

So when Jaden and Lori were really hyper and excited about bringing in the New Year as they waited for me to tell them what to recount, I grew quiet.

And when Lori didn't stop talking about her boyfriend Greg I really wanted to roll my eyes. While we were counting, she told us how she was leaving the university she'd worked so hard to get into instead to study at a community college for this boyfriend who recently cheated on her, and yet all she was doing was waiting for him to call and say "Happy New Year" from his Mexico vacation. When Greg finally called, her persona completely changed. Her confidence at that moment was going to be entirely determined by how successful their phone call was. Then she talked to his mom, and when she got off the phone Lori told us how she's been in so many fights with Greg's mom. It's moments like that one where I wish some people could hear themselves and how ridiculous they sound to the world around them.

We finally finished all we could with inventory, and Jaden volunteered to shut the movie projectors off. Lori and I were hanging in the office.

"Do you think Greg and I will work out?" Lori randomly asked me.

I gave her an answer that I don't think anyone ever had before because I later found out that she brought it up to Jaden when they were walking to their cars.

"I don't know, Lori," I said. Lori and I were friends; we had worked together for a long time. But it's not like

I knew her life. We didn't go to the same high schools, and I only knew what she told me about their relationship and what I heard from other co-workers and friends. "I just don't want to see you get hurt. You know Greg should support you in where *you* want to go to school; you shouldn't have to come back here for him. If he's that good of a guy he'd want you to be where *you* want to be."

If anyone knows the truth can hurt, it's me, but I believe there's a difference between being mean and being honest. I've seen way too many people settle for less than fantastic relationships, and it drives me nuts. Sometimes I wish I could just shake my friends and say, "What are you *doing* with this person?!" It can be so obvious to outsiders when two people aren't meant for each other, or when one is tormenting the other; but why is it that the other falls for it?

The same thing occurred for way too long with my friends Hannah and Patrick. It seemed over half the time they were together there was unnecessary drama. They were both at different places in their lives; Hannah was just figuring out high school, while Patrick was ready to go off to college. They had different frustrations and issues to tackle, and after a while one person's problems were just another person's eye rolls. Patrick felt tied down, and Hannah had so many other dilemmas to focus on that a boyfriend didn't make matters better. They came down to the point where there were multiple times they discussed breaking up, and finally I believe it was Patrick who called it off after *two years* of this commotion.

That was kind of a crazy time in both of their lives; Patrick was in college, finally feeling some freedom to breathe and figure out himself, and Hannah had made the rash decision to transfer to another high school.

I had dinner with Hannah in October of our junior year. I hadn't seen her since she and Patrick ended, so I was definitely curious to hear how things were going. And I couldn't believe how *great* life was for her now. Hannah was *finally* happy, and I could see it in her entire persona. She told me about how she felt this big lift off her shoulders when the relationship was done, and she had seemed to find herself again. Hannah at last had realized that their relationship didn't make either of them better people; it was just a big strain. That dinner was one of those times where afterwards I drove home thinking, *Wow, life might actually work out for some of us after all.*

You know that couple in your life who are always on-again-off-again? Or what about those two people who have only stressed themselves out since one of them went off to college? Or that girl who didn't go after what she really wanted because she didn't want to stray away from her boyfriend? We all know those types, and maybe some of you are those types. My question then is this: Why?

If there is one phrase that will forever remain true about love it is the fact that love is blind. I think this is the one fact that people who have been single for a long time or have never been with anyone notice the most about people in relationships, because it is so freaking easy for someone on the outside, constantly using their noggin and not their heart, to notice. I feel people stay in bad relationships because they often think it's better to be living in pain with someone than to be alone…in other words, to be in my singular situation. But I will tell you that reason is completely backwards. Since I haven't been committed to anyone, I am able to do what I want. I can be really involved with extra-curricular activities, practice my interests, and travel. Shouldn't you be able to still do those things if you're with someone?

Obviously when you commit to someone, that relationship becomes something you set time aside for, save money for, and think about constantly. Just like I care about my performance in the activities I'm involved with, a person cares about the success of their relationship with someone. I really want to travel in the next upcoming years, and I hope that involves moving all around the United States and possibly even eventually visiting different parts of the world. It's easy for me to decide this because I don't have much holding me back. But what if I had a boyfriend? What would he say? Well, after everything I've observed, I would hope the guy I decide to commit to would say, "Go for it." I am so excited to see this world through my own eyes; it's been a dream of mine for a very long time. Traveling is what I believe will make me a better person, because every travel experience I've had so far already has. If I was with someone who said to me, "Stacey, I need to travel for the next year to learn more about myself and to fulfill a couple dreams I've always had," I would do two things:

cry and smile. I'd be sad that my man was going to be away from me for so long, but I would support him and his dreams. If this is what he needed to do for him, and maybe even for our relationship to continue growing, then I would believe in it, too. I hope this is the way your partner looks at your relationship and vice versa.

This is why Lori's relationship made me feel bad for her, and why I'm honestly so thankful Hannah and Patrick didn't last. Lori wasn't looking out for herself in her relationship; she was only doing what would please Greg. Going to community college for Greg was not going to make Lori a better person, if anything it would just make her resent him. And truthfully it's quite selfish of Greg to never have said, "No, you need to stay where you are and we will work through this." Hannah and Patrick finally reached a place where their relationship was more work than joy. When they were finally done, they realized they were allowed to make goals and actually act on them without anyone nagging them for it.

I believe love should be easy. A relationship of course is never going to be smooth sailing, but even in the middle of a fight, you shouldn't resent or hate your person. Lori gave in by coming back home for Greg, and Hannah and Patrick gave in for two years too long. There shouldn't be any discussions of whether of not you should break up in a good relationship. There shouldn't be any settling on your part. There should only be growth, support, love, and trust. When I say that though, I understand that it is very easy for people who have been in relationships to say to me, "You've never been in a relationship, you don't know how it is." Well isn't growth, support, love, and trust exactly what you believed in before you met your partner? Isn't that why you signed the contract? At the end of the day, love *should* be easy. A *relationship* is not easy, but if love is there, *love* will be easy. Growth, support, love, and trust are the components in a bond between two people that make each other better individuals. Therefore you should be able to do what you dream of doing along with being committed to someone; at least, I believe that you should. If your person cares enough about your individual progression as a human being, then they will believe in you and cheer you on. But if they aren't willing to believe in what you want, in what you value, then what's the point of trying to impress them? They're making you frustrated because they don't care about your needs, so go find someone who will care.

And now I'll finally tell you about Sean.

Let's review; Sean was the first guy I ever wore sweatpants in front of and no makeup (that is a big deal). He was my friend and someone I could always rely on; he *always* listened. Sean taught me the idea of companionship in a relationship versus just finding Prince Charming. I wanted to date him, but he wasn't ready and often avoided the subject. So we remained good friends.

Then I went off to study abroad for a year and bitch Morgan entered Sean's life.

I'm not the type to tell anyone who'll listen that someone's a bitch, but Morgan is the exception. She is the clearest definition of a significant other who only brings someone down and not up. Don't worry, I've already told her all of this, so she knows. The Sean I knew was someone who never once asked me to walk to his house to hang; he automatically assumed to pick me up at my dorm. The Sean I knew texted me just to say good night even if we hadn't talked all week. When I knew Sean, he was both tough and soft. And he cared—my God, did he care about his friends. But he allowed Morgan to change all of that.

Sean evolved into the guy who didn't go to the bar with his friends because his girlfriend said he couldn't, even though she went out with her friends. He got a matching tattoo with this chick on his wrist just months after dating her. He got a fucking Great Dane puppy with this girl (Great Dane puppies grow into Great Dane full-sized dogs if you were wondering)! Sean let Morgan walk all over him, and he almost got away from it all when he broke up with her in the middle of the school year...plus he told me he regretted not dating me (though I was long over that shit by then). Sean realized I would've been, um, *good* to him, unlike Morgan. But then she conned him back in, making him believe they were good for each other. And then he dropped out of college for a semester, and his life became really messed up for a while. I told Sean I couldn't be friends with him when he's disrespecting himself by keeping Morgan in his life, but I still got countless midnight texts from him saying he was sorry. I never replied until the summer when I realized I wasn't allowing him to get past this to perhaps put his life back together. So I talked, but I didn't let him back in.

When I returned to school after studying abroad for a year, we hung out twice. And Morgan found out, and like she always does, flipped out on Sean.

I was doing homework when Morgan Facebook messaged me "How many times have you and Sean seen each other". Moments later Sean had me on speakerphone to tell Morgan that we didn't have sex (which we DID NOT). My friend of four years, needed *me* to tell *his* girlfriend that he didn't cheat on her. After Sean hung up on me, I replied to Morgan's Facebook message…and I gave it to her straight.

Her response?

"You don't know me or this relationship."

For the record, when I told you a couple paragraphs before this that Morgan's response is exactly how people in relationships often respond to this whole topic, I wrote that two years before any of this ever happened with Morgan.

My response to her?

"I think Sean telling me all about your fights this past year, him dropping out of school for a semester, and the fact that no one I know has ever said anything positive about you or your relationship is a good indicator that I know *enough*."

She never replied.

I realized that Sean's nerve to put his old friend's voice on the line right in between his pathetic relationship was enough of an indicator to know this friendship was done; Sean wasn't a *friend* to me. I haven't talked to him since.

I'm not telling you this so I can call out Morgan (although I don't mind that part), I'm trying to show you what a situation can turn into when you let your significant other take control of your life, twist your thoughts about yourself, and take you to a place your former self knew better than to be in. Everyone I've talked to about Sean has said he's changed since Morgan came into his life, and not for the better. And you might also notice from this story that Sean lost a good friend from this bad relationship. I didn't want him to dump Morgan so I could be his girlfriend; I wanted my friend to get his life back on track. Your friends should like your significant other. The reason your friends *will* like your significant other is because they can see how this person makes you happier. I never saw that in Sean after Morgan entered his life; all he ever said was he knew he needed to end it, but then he never did. I don't know how that makes for a good relationship. Morgan does not make Sean a better person; not even a little.

I know it's easier said than done, especially if you've forgotten what it's like to be single, but if your significant other doesn't make you grow into a better person, leave them. Don't ever think you have to stay in a relationship with someone who doesn't build you up, and don't fear that if you leave you won't find something better. It might take some time, but you will most definitely find someone better than the dirt bag who does nothing good for your life. Find someone who will believe in your dreams and make you chase after them. You should be allowed to continue being you, and then grow into a better you, once you commit to someone.

Love is respect.

I am in no place to speak about what one should do in a relationship where they are getting abused, other than you should tell someone and get help. But I do know from the family life I was brought up with that love is *respect*— jealousy, mistrust, settling, fear, and dishonesty do not qualify as love. When someone loves you, they make you feel safe, secure, happy, and open to express yourself. Love always has been and always will be *respect*, and if this is not how you feel in a relationship get out and move on. There are many shapes and forms of disrespect in a relationship that can make a person feel hurt. Sadly sometimes it is abuse, but many times it is simply a feeling that things are always rocky, topsy-turvy, or like you have no idea what the next day will bring to challenge you. I believe that two people do not have a committed, successful relationship going if there is enough of this toxicity between them.

I haven't ever been anyone's center of his world, but I know that in any area of life, in any relationship a person has with another human being, love means respect in every culture and on every place in this world. You don't go into a relationship willing to accept bullshit from someone. A relationship is supposed to make you feel happy about yourself, not sad or depressed. Love is knowing that yes, maybe your boyfriend is surrounded by other girls at work or in his classes, but he loves *you*; if he is that good of a person then those surrounding girls don't mean a thing to him. Love is cheering your person on to do something they love, and encouraging them when they don't believe in themselves. It's opening the car door for your lady or asking if everything's okay when it's obviously not. On the other hand, respect for your significant other is *not* flirting with other girls, sending or getting drunk texts every night, making your guy stay in all the time, bailing on each other, or one person always making more effort...needless to say, respect goes both ways in a relationship.

I might still be single, but I have had my heart broken before. If anyone thinks that a person who has never had somebody to share their life with feels no pain, they are wrong. It's heartbreak on a whole different level, and what's horrible about it is it makes you mad at the world rather than just one person. Depending how the evil spirit of loneliness bites you, it can make a person despise every couple they see, it can turn them away from their faith, or it can just make them give up on the world. It's one thing to have a sad break up that changes your life, but it's another to watch everyone else have what you would give anything for. I've watched a lot of people take their significant other for granted, which is even more annoying. And it makes me wonder why would anyone want to be with someone who uses him or her, or makes him or her feel like crap? I know that feeling of heartbreak, and it is horrible to go through. But to put yourself through heartbreak when you are *in* a relationship defeats the whole purpose of being in one. Love is respect, not jealousy or frustration, and if there's any hatred or sadness in the relationship I don't know how anyone can decide it's still okay to stay romantically involved with that person (Unless it's a situation where a person fears they'll be in danger if they leave; again, that is an abusive situation and you must tell someone so you can seek help.).

This is the part where I wanted to simply say that I am not the resource you should be seeking if you're in an abusive relationship. I've been fortunate enough to be raised in an environment where a great family has always loved me, and so I know that love is not a competitive game of making each other miserable. It's a commitment in working together to build the best life possible. Your significant other shouldn't be making you jealous with their friends or lifestyle, and neither person in a relationship should feel like they're only hanging on by a thread. That's not fair, and it breaks trust. Jealousy and mistrust ruin so many relationships. Love is supposed to make us all happy, not hurt. Respect keeps us going, not feeling hopeless. If you are in a relationship that only makes you feel upset and worthless, then get out; because even if it takes as long as it's taking me to find love, being single still feels better than being with someone who only makes you unhappy. Love is respect; don't forget that.

If you or someone you know needs help in getting out of

an abusive relationship, tell someone or log on to loveisrespect.org.

Ladies, your man is allowed to have friends of the opposite sex.

Boys can definitely be dumb and shy, but girls can be absolutely irrational. This is most often found when girls become obsessive of their boyfriends. Boys, this is the part where I'm totally on your side; obsessive girlfriends are so unattractive.

Towards the end of my friend Andrea's relationship with Garrett, she was constantly asking me about how much Garret was talking to other girls. Garrett had a past with two other girls in our high school, and they all happened to be in one of my classes together. But by this time in our high school careers these flings Garrett had had with these two girls were long over, and both of the girls were in long-term relationships. All these facts, though, didn't stand a chance in stopping Andrea from feeling paranoid that Garrett was checking out those other two girls in class. Andrea was constantly asking me questions like "Did he talk to them today? How much does he talk to them? Does he flirt with them?" I always reassured her she was making it all up in her head, because literally nothing flirty was going on between the three in my class.

"I know I sound crazy asking this stuff all the time, but it bugs me so much every time I see Garrett around them," Andrea would say.

While I understood because I am a girl, I also believed Andrea had nothing to worry about.

My other friend Rachel had a lot of the same issues with her boyfriend Drew. When they were together, Rachel and Drew were in a long distance relationship. Drew was very involved on his college campus and was totally one of those guys who has a lot of girl friends, simply because he's a genuine person who cares about everyone. Facebook though did not help in calming Rachel's overanalyzing about this. Rachel couldn't stand the thought of Drew being around other girls, even though they were thousands of miles away from one another, and frankly there was nothing she could do about it. It wasn't Drew she didn't trust but rather the girls around him.

Ladies, settle down. You man is allowed to have friends who are girls, just as much as you can have friends who are guys.

I hate how girls often make the next guy that comes along pay for the last douche bag's mistakes. Every girl is going to fall for an idiot who breaks her heart, but ladies we will also fall for guys who are good people, and *won't* cheat on you (I personally know more guys who would never even think about cheating than guys who would). Your boyfriend is allowed to talk and joke around with females. If you can have a night out with your girls, he can do the same with his buddies. You have to believe and remember he likes *you* and won't cheat; it's part of something called trust. Yes, there's a good chance some girl at the bar will come up to him and start flirting with him, but if he's a good guy he won't take that chick home. Don't be that annoying, crazy obsessive girl, and if you are that girl maybe you should look into why you feel that way; it could be because there is an issue in your relationship that needs to be addressed, or it could be because you yourself are not a trusting girlfriend.

I have hung out with close guy friends of mine who were in relationships, and guess what– nothing happened between us and everyone survived. For example I have two great friends, Ren and Austin, and I was close with each of them separately long before they got together. So once they started dating, I started hoping I wasn't going to lose my friendship with Austin just because he was dating Ren. Austin and I had hung out zillions of times just us before Ren was his girlfriend, and he is like a brother to me. Ren understands that because she and Austin trust each other. Austin and I still got to hang out every once in a while on our own. As Austin's friend, I was happy I could still hang with him, and as Ren's friend, I was appreciative that she knew neither Austin nor I would cross those boundaries.

Boys, you should know if you haven't already figured it out, that girls overthink *everything*. Like, *everything*. It's just how we are, it doesn't do us much good, but it's never going to change. But ladies, your guy is allowed to still be friends with the girls he was friends with before you two got together, and he's even allowed to become friends with girls after you two get together. He's not going to cheat on you if he's a good guy; he likes *you*. Don't be that obsessive girl; she's so annoying.

There's no "I" in team.

I think high-fives are a really sexy thing between two significant others. Of course a hug and a kiss are the ultimate high, but there's something to be said about a couple who can high-five it out, too. There's as much friendship in that as there is love. It enthusiastically means *I'm by your side, I trust you, and I believe in us, but you're also my buddy and my partner-in-crime*. Maybe that's taking the idea of a hand slap a little far, but these are the types of things I notice. These are the little details I want for my own love story one day.

This idea reminds me a lot of my parents' relationship and marriage. Tom and Karen have been married for twenty-five years now, and I think they're a little bit of one of those "can't live with them, can't live without them" couples. The older they get the more hilarious they are. I remember when I still lived at home often waking up on a Saturday morning, hearing them talking before they got out of bed and laughing their asses off about God knows what. And then in the afternoon they're always attacking some project with the house or the grocery list. They constantly have a plan; Wednesday night Tom's off so they'll take his car to the body shop; Karen can cook something in the oven Sunday night, and Tom will grill on Monday. Of course they have arguments, what couple doesn't; but I've always noticed how *easy* their relationship is. I don't mean the taking the kids to school and balancing life part; I mean their relationship as partners. There's no question with their love for each other, and I think this truly is because they are a team. They have a system in place. They compromise, but at the end they do it to gain something else. My parents' teamwork is why I'm so blessed to be in this family; it's endlessly stable.

I feel like everyone relates teamwork to relationships; relationships of any sort, really. Well here's the thing; no, there's no "I" in TEAM, however I think people tend to forget this a lot. If there isn't teamwork between a man and a woman, then they're still a boy and a girl. Teamwork is certainly easier said than done; it's a process to learn. But if you believe your person is worth signing the contract for, then you're going to have to learn how to master this word. My parents understand teamwork; however they've had over a quarter of a century to learn it. But what about first-time parents, newlyweds, people who have just moved in together, two high school sweethearts going away to separate colleges? I think from day one with someone teamwork is absolutely essential.

I feel teamwork is a process that honestly starts before you're even officially dating a person. When I look at my life the one word that comes to mind is *control,* and this I know will always be an issue for me. I am a control freak! I'm a leader, I'm a perfectionist, and every detail of whatever I'm involved with has to be planned and prepared. To some degree, I know a person has to let go in a relationship, yet this is so hard for me to do. I've had too many people fail to complete tasks up to my ideals, so I'm used to saying "If you want something done right, do it yourself." However, you can't say this in a relationship. Where's the magic in that? I pray to God that I never become one of those old married couples in which one of the people in the relationship is completely whipped by the other. There are control issues in a situation like that, and people shouldn't be scared to stand up for themselves amidst their bond. I don't want to be in charge of a relationship, but I also don't want to be a trophy wife. That said, there also cannot be anyone lazy in a relationship. I saw a quote on Pinterest that said *I want to hear a guy say "I made plans for us," instead of "I dunno, whatever you want to do I guess."* I couldn't have said it better.

Teamwork is a tricky thing to talk about, because it's all about balance and commitment in all shapes and forms. The only reason I feel qualified to discuss teamwork as a single girl is because I've seen so many people fail at it and wonder what went wrong in their relationship, or I've seen people know they're not doing their part and walk away anyways. I believe there are two types of teamwork that a couple needs to master: the everyday teamwork, and the life teamwork.

After seeing people date and my own minimal dating

experience, I decided there are two kinds of teamwork in relationships: the everyday teamwork, and the life teamwork. You need both to keep a relationship going, equally from both people, in both areas. There's always going to be the challenge of keeping a balance between the little things like who's turn it is to do the laundry, but then there's also the challenge of finding a way to fit each other happily into your lives while still accomplishing your dreams (and I say dreams because your person should support *dreams,* not just goals). *Everything* in a relationship takes teamwork, and I don't know if a person can really find success in love until they realize this.

I feel everyday teamwork is basically everything involved with staying in communication with each other; and this is where I think Brad and I failed. We discussed our goals and places we wanted to see a million times, but we screwed up the everyday check-ins. Rather than saying things like "How are you?" "I'm doing okay, how are you?" it would be this:

(Brad) "Calculus is kicking my ass. I'm so drained from school."

(Stacey) "Yeah, I'm feeling really overwhelmed with homework and my roommate's driving me nuts."

(Brad) "I'm just ready to graduate."

(Stacey) "I just want to go travel."

Do you see the difference or am I just nuts? I think we were both constantly waiting for the other person to ask about *us,* but the other would never get the hint, or perhaps we did get the hint but just kept talking about ourselves. In the beginning with Brad when I hadn't quite been aware of how hectic his schedule was (not that mine was any better) anytime I messaged him and didn't get a reply I went mental inside. Of course I didn't want Brad to see this freaked out part of me. I wanted to support him and let him vent to me, but I wanted that back from him, too. I also didn't want to come off as some little freshman who was always available whenever he wanted. If Brad wanted this thing between us to become a relationship, then all I wanted was for him to say "I'm working till late tonight I'll text you after"; just *something* so I knew it wasn't because of me!

See all that ridiculousness right there? *That's* why you need everyday teamwork! Here's the thing: boys are dumb and girls are crazy. Boys can't take a hint and girls overanalyze absolutely everything. So boys, a little notification of why you're not texting as much will make your future lives a lot easier, and girls, boys don't know what the hell they're doing, so don't think they're a step ahead of you! If a guy hasn't messaged you all day odds are it's because he was at basketball practice or work and then went to his buddy's house to play Xbox; Don't. Freak. Out.

Whether you've just started dating someone or are in a serious relationship, you need everyday teamwork to keep things steady. If you hate setting the table, then clear after dinner. If he likes to grill then you make something tasty in the oven. If you're freaking out that he didn't call you, talk to him and just say "It's not that I'm trying to stalk your life, but when I'm used to hearing from you at 10 P.M. and I don't I freak out a little inside. I know I shouldn't but I do. Can you just let me know if you're not going to be available so I don't have to wonder why you're not responding to my text?" That way your person is aware of the fact that you know you're absolutely insane in the head, but you're trying to be semi-normal and work with them.

Along with the business-type everyday teamwork of housework and communication, there's also got to be everyday teamwork in the romance department! This is the part where I share with you some of my hopes for my future relationship as if we're a couple of giggly seventh grade girls at a sleepover with popcorn and Kool-Aid. I hope one day for good night text messages with smiley face emoticons, a guy who has enough balls to call me instead of text me, someone who just listens to my issues and says it's okay and that I'm not as crazy as I feel, someone who calls me out when I'm unfair, a go-getter who knows how to reserve a table at a nice restaurant, and someone who has a life besides me and yet looks forward to a date night once a week and movie nights whenever possible. I would do and be all these things for my person in a heartbeat. It takes teamwork to keep romance alive, but the romance part of the everyday teamwork is like the sprinkles on your favorite ice cream in June.

I think we've covered everyday teamwork pretty well; now on to life teamwork.

The differences between everyday teamwork and life teamwork are kind of ironic: if everyday teamwork isn't

WHAT I'VE LEARNED FROM NEVER HAVING A *Boyfriend*

going well, we kind of just try to ignore the fact that it is failing and keep things going with the person. But if there's a vast difference between two people's life situations, people run the other direction if it makes life teamwork difficult. Wouldn't you think it would be the other way around? We fall for people because we fall in love with their interests, passions, and dreams. We try to become a part of the life they've always imagined.

I know I will have trouble with life teamwork. What am I doing between now and until the day I am in a relationship? Planning for a career.

I've been around the country now, and I can say guys vary according to location, as I'm sure girls do, too. And what I've discovered is I really do like a good midwestern boy. However, Midwest guys want to build a house in some small Midwest town. There's nothing wrong with that at all; part of me would love the type of life where there's grass, wholesome families, and a slower pace...but not at this time in my life. That's not my kind of dream. I want the polar opposite: a New York apartment that doesn't have roaches and a fulfilling career in writing and film. Guys in the Midwest are genuine, hard working, beer drinking boys who love their moms. But a guy like that usually doesn't want to move to New York, and I would regret every day I didn't move to a city if I decided to stay back for a guy in the Midwest.

This is where I tell the individual who has big dreams to wait on a boyfriend. Think of every girl you know who's only been single for about five seconds since she was thirteen; she has never had time to discover her own identity. Think of that nice guy we all know who only thought about having a girlfriend in high school but never got it; did he ever take time to realize he should figure out himself before he tries to impress a girl? Part of the reason I haven't been in a relationship yet is because I fear losing myself in a relationship. I've seen this happen to too many girls, and they end up left in pieces. It has nothing to do with the guy; it's about me, not them! I can think of the times I've turned a guy down and suddenly felt this sense of relief upon myself. *Well, I'm back to square one, but I'm also at a place where I'm comfortable,* I would think. If I'm going to be with someone, I'm going to be one hundred percent committed; I'm an all-or-nothing person.

This whole idea is why I believe in the importance of life teamwork. Of course you will compromise in a relationship; you have to. But should you completely give up your dreams for someone else's? Absolutely not. Therefore, to a certain degree, you have to find someone who has the same desires and dreams as you do. If you're in love with the high school varsity football player who will work for the family business in the same town for the rest of his life and you want New York, then honey, you've got to move on. I do not think it's wrong, by any means, to date different people when you're my age to figure these things out though! In high school or college it is definitely a good idea to date different people to see what you do and don't like. I love the idea of growing old up north with some Midwest guy, but it doesn't coordinate with my city dreams. So I have to find someone who will. With life teamwork, you do have to be semi-similar with a person in values and goals. You have to be able to build each other up to go after what you both want, and yet be able to stand by your person's side at their finish line. You can't do this if your boyfriend is growing corn and soybeans in Wisconsin and you're modeling in Miami. But if you can find a guy who wants to backpack Europe like you do, then maybe he's worth a shot.

There's as much attention to detail as there is focus on the big picture when it comes to teamwork; it's a dance of balancing big dreams with everyday realities. I will say though, if I can have a marriage like my parents', a relationship where there's a plan about who's going to kill ladybugs, who's going to do dishes, plus how and where we're going to grow old together, then I'd say it's worth the search for the right person to be my star teammate. I'd high-five that.

Boys with sisters tend to have their shit together.

I truly believe that the more females a man grows up with, the more he will be in tuned with what we ladies love, hate, and cry about. For example, I have a friend named Vince, who has four women in his house, and he is such an amazing husband to Dawn. They have been together since high school, and they are one of those couples that are electric to be around. Vince is one of those guys who I know would always give me great advice about guys when we were in high school. If I told him a guy dilemma, he could explain to me the differences between males and females so much so that we could pin point where things were going sour with my issues. I honestly challenge you to think of the guys you know who are fantastic boyfriends. How many sisters do they have? If you know they grew up with a number of females in their household, consider it your lucky day.

This theory certainly doesn't mean that there aren't any great guys out there who grew up with a male dominant household; I also know guys who were very close to their moms and are just as fantastic of guys like Vince. However, I have noticed from some guys who have grown up with several brothers that things are more rough-and-tough and black and white with them. There aren't always the subtle hints of romanticism like holding the door for a girl, buying her flowers, pushing in her chair, sensing when she's moody, etc., and these are things Vince always was quick to pick up on. Girls pay a *tremendous* amount of attention to detail, and they want the guy to get the hint that she wants to cuddle or hold hands. Many times guys need these hints to be as smooth as a slap in the face, but I feel the men who grow up around females have been whipped into shape and are often ahead of the game in the love department.

*There's a difference between
a marriage and a wedding day.*

My friend Rachel is obsessed with weddings…like *obsessed*. I've never really been one to plan my wedding, but this girl has it all figured out. Rachel is in love with France; therefore it is her dream to get married in a French chateau…in France. It will only cost around forty thousand dollars, and if she gets married in France she *has* to have a Cartier wedding ring. However, if she must settle to getting married in the United States, she will get a Tiffany ring.

When we lived in the dorms together Rachel and I one night were watching T.V. and surfing the web when Rachel showed me the wedding ring she wants on Cartier's website. As I'm sure my facial expression screamed *what the hell,* I nodded and said "nice". Then Rachel continued to tell me how many karats this ring was, the price, ya da ya da ya da.

"I've never been on the Cartier or Tiffany websites," I said casually while pinning away on Pinterest.

The room became silent. If looks could kill, Rachel would be on a most wanted list right now.

"You've. Never. Been. On. These. Sites?"

"Nope," I replied.

Guess I'm crazy.

Often when people bring up the idea of weddings, I

joke I'm just going to go to the courthouse, get the papers signed, and call it a day. The idea of planning a wedding makes me want to pull my hair out. Every now and then I'll mention something about my wedding day to my dad, and his response always is "Well, first you gotta get a boyfriend!" with a good chuckle following.

I really don't plan my wedding. I never have; I've always just thought it's something I should do with my fiancé. I have ideas, but not *plans*. I didn't think this was an issue until that night with Rachel, but this moment also made me realize how much emphasis some people truly put on this one day in their lives.

I am at an age now where my friends are starting to get engaged, and I know within the coming years, I will have many weddings to attend. I absolutely love weddings; I love dressing up, I look forward to approving Snapchats of what my friends want to wear to the ceremony, I take advantage of the free food and alcohol, I love deciding if the bride's dress looks good or not, and most of all I love dancing the night away to oldies tunes with people twice my age who are the least bit sober (c'mon, who doesn't?). In other words, weddings freaking rock. You get to party on someone else's dime all the while believing again that love really does exist when you see the bride and groom unite in *marriage*– you know, that one little word, that means "till death do us part"?

Weddings are great, but I think people sometimes mix up the meanings between *wedding* and *marriage*, so let's clarify: *wedding* means one day of your life where you dress up and make a promise to someone that you will be their one and only, every single day, no matter if they go bald, gain fifty pounds, lose their sex drive three years down the road, experience a mid-life crisis, all until the day you croak. *Marriage* means actually living out that promise. I personally feel there's a slight difference amid those two words, but some how that miniscule variance often gets forgotten amongst the planning of ceremony locations, accent colors, and guest lists.

People today rush insanely fast towards finding success, and for many that includes finding a spouse and popping out some kids before hitting age thirty. People want that glorious moment we see through television, music, and social media everyday. We want that white-picket fence dream home we bought for Barbie dolls twenty years ago to be real, and we want it now. So many people go and get it; they marry their high school sweetheart because that's the only relationship they've ever known, or they search high and low for Mr. Right in whatever college setting they land in. And after two years of dating, everyone's asking about wedding rings, so the guy gets down on one knee and proposes. And the girl says yes, and suddenly it's all about making those wedding pins on Pinterest a reality, finding that perfect barn or beach setting and mapping out every single pose that has to be photographed of you and your fiancé. And despite the stress and the expenses, this wedding is all the bride has ever thought about, so before you know it the day is here and you're saying, "I do." And then you settle down together, and people start asking, "When are you going to have a baby?" So you get pregnant, and nine months later half of you is genetically coded into a little seven-pound human being that cries and poops constantly. So there you are after two years of dating, a year of wedding planning, a day of a wedding, and maybe two years after that with a newborn to feed, a spouse to keep happy even though by now you're probably tired as hell, a new mortgage to pay, and a job to work where you're likely still at the bottom of the totem pole in your position…all at the tender of age of what, twenty-five?

So, now what?

At twenty-five years old, you have been able to drink legally for four years and buy cigarettes, tobacco, and tattoos for seven years, but now you can rent a car, you can run to be elected into the House of Representatives, and all the while you still can be on your parents' health insurance! Instead though, you chose to give a lot of that up for a marriage, a kid, a house, and maybe even a minivan. There's nothing wrong with that decision, and I must say it does really resemble my Barbie mansion setup back in the day, but now I'm going to ask you this: are you happy? Is this new life of yours after sampling wedding cakes and pairing bridesmaids and groomsmen together exactly what you envisioned? Is this what the big picture of your life looked like when you pictured yourself in your mid-twenties, or was there something else you never got around to before the proposal?

We focus so much attention on the big picture of our goals; but that's what causes us frustration when we're not at the place we recognize as happiness. If we take more time to appreciate the little things, we could solve this problem we all face, and essentially "find happy," as I like to call it.

I'm personally really not good at being exceedingly happy; I'm definitely not always feeling perfectly balanced or in love with life. In all honesty, I'm not in a bright mood about ninety percent of the time. I'm either tired or stressed, and the few times I'm neither, I don't know what to do with this whole "happy" thing. And it's kind of ridiculous because happiness is what we all strive for. We date to find someone who makes us happy. We get married to find happy. We make sure absolutely every detail of our wedding day is perfect to find happy, and we work our tails off to build a life with this person we're head over heels about to be happy.

I think finding happy is so simple it's complicated. Finding happy isn't just those moments of achievement in our lives, like our wedding day. We focus so much attention on ideas like "When I'm in a relationship I'll be happy," "When I'm married I'll be happy," "When I have a home filled with kids I'll be happy." So if this is what we all strive for, how come once we supposedly get there, we're not always feeling as happy as we intended to? Or what happens when we don't achieve these hopes and dreams by the age we thought we would? What happens to finding happy then? Is it really just gone when we feel a rush of defeat instead?

Personally, I'm really tough on myself when it comes to finding happy. I want it all; I want the best. But I've really learned through the things I love like cinema, traveling, and memorable moments that "happy" is simply those everyday little things. In order to be happy in a relationship, the little things are what we need to focus on. Some of us won't meet our dream guy in college like we thought we would, and some of us will be the last one pregnant amongst all our girlfriends; that's just how life works out. I certainly never planned on being single this long, but here I am, and I make the best of it even though it can be really frustrating. I'll be honest, people with life stories about leadership, perseverance, and self-discovery fascinate me ten times more than relationship stories; if the first thing you tell me about yourself is something about your boyfriend, I'm judging you. I can relate so much more to the journey of learning about oneself than I can with falling in love and discovering oneself through another person. To some people being single sounds terrifying, but it's usually not the end of the world…actually it never has been in my experience.

What I'm trying to say is if you only try to find happy in the next thing you're after, like a wedding day, you probably never will. I can't tell you how to find happy because that's different for everyone, but I can tell you after having constantly putting myself out there to meet and impress new people wherever I go, that marriage and babies cannot be rushed. You have to focus on what's in front of you right now, whether that's single life or growing a strong bond with a significant other. If you're in a relationship that you believe could turn into a marriage, then work on building that foundation *now* while you're dating rather than depending on the idea that it will all come into place when you're married with a baby at twenty-five years old. If it's not strong now, a mortgage and a little pooping human won't make it any better.

While a wedding day is filled with beautiful moments, it's *one day*, whereas there's a lifetime of marriage after. In the ratio of wedding to marriage, wedding is the material item and marriage is the moment, and in a world where divorce is evermore accepted as a solution to a mess of a relationship, it's time that we enforce the idea of building a strong bond with someone before we hear any ringing of wedding bells.

In today's day and age with TLC wedding shows, Pinterest engagement photos, and constant array of celebrities walking down the aisle, it's hard not to get caught up in French chateaus and Tiffany rings. I believe that I have grown up in a generation with the following kind of business mantra: *If they can make money on it, they will*, which also means that every item on this earth will be marketed precisely to the appropriate audience. I first realized this when I started looking for a prom dress; and then when I planned prom; and then when I could buy a class ring, buy my graduation cap and gown, even when I went to college and my parents got a letter in the mail about lame overpriced care packages they could buy for my ass! It's extremely ridiculous, and kind of disgusting, too. It's no wonder we have those bridezilla shows and why people get divorced after seventy-two days of marriage; cake toppers and color palettes become more important than the person you walk down the aisle to. I'm not trying to be a fun-sucker for every girl who dreams of their wedding day; but don't start planning who's going to be your bridesmaids on the first date with someone. *Marriage* and *wedding* do not have the same meaning. Yes, we all picture the wedding day, but it's so important that we think about life beyond that.

Life goes on after the big day.

I've also noticed how relationships vary from one couple to another after the wedding day; while I'd say everyone seems to be in bliss to some degree, some are more than others. The couples who live together or have been together for ten years are much calmer after their wedding day. I would guess that this is not really how most girls intend or expect to be feeling after the biggest day of their lives, but I think it is something that often occurs. Like we all thought prom was going to change our lives, we expect the same for our wedding day; and yes, obviously your life is a little different the day after you say your vows, but you are the same person and your partner is the same person even when you're officially husband and wife. So if you don't actually picture *forever* with your fiancé, you should know that your life is supposed to continue on with them after the ceremony and reception (shocker I know).

Part of the reason I want to wait so long with

marriage is because I fear that point I think every couple eventually reaches; that moment when you look at each other, one of you has baby spit-up on you and the other is going bald, and you ask yourselves "Who are we?" A family friend once said to me, "You know that seven-year itch they talk about with marriage? Well, it exists," after telling me how much her husband had been getting on her nerves. I don't want to reach that point when you realize you and your person are kind of boring. Of course nobody does, but then why do so many people become "old married couples" before they know it? What happens then when you're twenty-five, married with kids? You have your whole life to be married, and unless you keep things exciting, I don't see the point in walking down the aisle so early. You only get one wedding, so why would you want it to be over before you know it, and your kids will love you no matter what age you are. I just think life should be exciting, and marriage is all about settling down. It's not that marriage is lame, but it seems to be the time when life catches up with you and either reminds you of everything you've accomplished or never did. Which way do you want to feel a year after saying "I do"?

I don't care if you think I'm a Debbie-Downer for saying these things; I've accepted who I am, so I just kind of tell it like it is if you haven't noticed. But this is something that I feel people in my generation just do not understand with marriage; it is *forever*. I don't like to use celebrities as examples since they seem to separate and get divorced so often, but Will Smith said a quote about marriage on *The Ellen Degeneres Show* that has always stuck with me (however note this quote doesn't pertain to anyone in an abusive relationship or situation).

"What I found is divorce just can't be an option," he said, "It's really that simple. A huge part of the success for [Jada] and I is that we just removed the other options."

Ever since I heard this quote I've had this perspective about marriage, and my aunt Amber told me something about her marriage that I'll also never forget. On the night of her wedding, she looked at her husband and said, "There's only one way to get out of this marriage: death."

If a couple rushes their relationship, they are going to lose their own personal identities. You're spending all this time focused on making this one thing a success between you and your partner, but you're going to forget your own values if you don't step back and evaluate everything once in a while. I think from day one of a relationship, you always have to remember to do your own check-ins with yourself. As you go through each stage with someone, you have to ask yourself, "Am I *honestly* happy with this phase we're in? Does this fit in to what I want to do with my life aside from our relationship?" I think this is when people will run into problems if they forget to do this. You can't sacrifice your own needs just to get to the next phase. If you're not ready to date someone, speak up. If you're not ready to move in with someone, say something. It's better to be honest right away, even if it does disappoint the other person; it will be a lot easier than bringing up the fact that you forgot to evaluate your feelings towards a situation when the rings are already on the fingers.

A family friend told me when I was younger that "If you have any doubt before walking down the aisle, *any doubt*, don't do it. Yes, it would be embarrassing to cancel a wedding, but this is your whole life you're committing to someone." I never forgot those words. You can't force someone to be ready for the next phase just because you already are, and you have to constantly ask yourself if you're happy, too. If you're ready to be a married twenty-five-year-old with two kids, then do it, but if you don't even want to think about that stuff until you're thirty-five then that's fine, too. You can't rush love; you can only make yourself the best you can be, and with that love, marriage, and babies will work their way into your life when they're supposed to.

Old parenting has its perks.

My parents have definitely demonstrated to me the benefits of waiting until you're a little bit older to marry and have kids. They dated for quite some time before they were engaged; something like three or four years, I believe. After they got married, I wasn't born until almost four years later. My mom was thirty and my dad thirty-seven when they had me. To some people, this is completely insane, and most people are shocked when I tell them my parents' ages today compared to my age. But I really think this is a great way to do the whole marriage and babies venture. I have heard numerous young women say they want to have kids young because they feel they'd be able to relate to them better; however, I don't think age has anything to do with *relating* to your kids. I relate perfectly to my parents; we have the same humor, we have the best of times when we're together, and they understand my issues.

I see more pros in being an older parent than a younger one. Here's why: my parents bought their first home when I was about four years old. I was around seventeen when the mortgage was paid off. Therefore they used the money they were originally using for the monthly mortgage payments and put it away into my college fund, *along* with what they had already saved for me over the years. A lot of my friends with younger parents had barely anything saved for school; my parents were able to pay for three of my college years on their own, of which I am entirely grateful for! Our house is quaint; it's not one of those $350,000 suburb homes you see rich bitches touring on *House Hunters*. Since my parents paid off the house mortgage relatively fast, we were also able to travel a lot as a family while Amanda and I were growing up, plus I went on tons of cross-country trips with school. My parents were also more established in their careers before they had kids, so when Amanda and I came along, there wasn't a *horrible* strain on how the bills were going to get paid.

My parents had experienced more than say the average married twenty-five-year-old with kids has by the time they started our family, like living in Milwaukee for instance. When I was born we were living on the south side of Milwaukee, which isn't the ghetto, but is certainly not a place where I enjoy getting out of my car. My dad would time how long it took my mom to walk me in my stroller around the block, and if she wasn't back in ten to fifteen minutes he would be out looking for her. There was even a drive-by shooting down the street from where we lived; some girl was killed because they were looking for her gangster boyfriend. Living in Milwaukee made my parents extremely protective of Amanda and I, despite how many times I reminded them that we lived in a town with a population of only two thousand people. However, that never mattered. When I wanted to go to the mall with my friends in fourth grade I couldn't go until they knew for sure that we were going to be supervised by an adult. When I wanted to go to National FFA Convention in Indianapolis with my FFA chapter in eighth grade they said no even though *all* my FFA friends were going. My dad completely bashed my idea to attend an out-of-state school straight out of high school, and don't even get me started on the time I asked if they would buy me beer for a party I was going to (I thought it was better to be upfront with them than to hide it!). Even after all this crazy protection, I'm thankful that my parents were so cautious. Sometimes I think back to some of the things my friends got to do at a younger age than me, and I realize my parents weren't that crazy after all; I don't know if I would let my kids do those same things either!

Lastly, my parents always have advice. I would say

this is the best thing about having parents thirty years your senior; they will always know the answer to your problems, whether it's what to do when your key breaks in half when you're trying to open your car in December (yes, it happened, sophomore year) or what to say when you've got to tell a clingy guy you went on a couple dates with that you can't be more than friends. My parents have always known when to tell me I can't do something, and today they understand that I'm an adult. They can only tell me the consequences of my actions, but *I* have to ultimately be the one to make choices for myself. My parents aren't my friends, they're my *parents;* that's something I think young parents don't always understand the difference between. Who knows, maybe I just had really great parents, but I really believe the fact that they are significantly older than me has something to do with it. I'm an old soul because of them, and proud of it.

Old love exemplifies true love.

The absolute best people to get love advice from are old people. Whether it's your grandparents, you neighbor, or nursing home patients, senior citizens are past all the B.S. of relationships, and they just *get* it. You can learn a lot from them, so when they have something to say, *listen*...more times than not, they're pretty spot on.

My grandparents on my mom's side got married young; my grandma was only eighteen when she married my grandpa. I ask them all the time to tell me about how they met. My grandma was with her girlfriends when my grandpa, who had just gotten out of the army, drove up in a fancy new car. If there's one thing you should know about my grandpa, it is that he *loves* cars. He started talking to my grandma and her friends. After she asked her parents, Grandma hopped in that car with Grandpa, and just like Grandma tells me, "they've been going together ever since." They've been together for over fifty-five years, and their love for each other inspires me. My grandma still misses him when Grandpa goes to the body shop or an auction for the day. They eat the same lunch everyday together; Grandma lays deli meat, sausage, and cheese out for sandwiches, and Grandpa eats a peanut butter sandwich every. single. day.

I could write another whole chapter about Grandpa and Grandma stories; one in particular is just classic. Grandma is that grandma who has the house decorated to the nines for every holiday, makes the most fantastic holiday dinners; everything is absolutely *pristine*. So of course this means that once dinner is done, the dishes are cleaned right away; however for Grandpa, dinner being complete means going into the living room with his toothpick and reading the paper. I'll never forget the time when Grandma was *finally* done with cleaning everything up. She came in the living room to join us. The moment she plopped down into her chair, Grandpa looked at her and asked, "Can I have my ice cream now?" Grandma paused, looked at me, got back up and made Grandpa his ice cream. Just thinking about it makes me laugh, but those are the kinds of moments that love is all about. Love is alive when your person does or says something crazy and you roll your eyes as you fall in love with them all over again; when you'll get back up after cooking dinner and cleaning dishes to make your spouse ice cream, just because you care that much about them.

My grandpa and grandma Springob, my dad's parents, seemed to have a very similar relationship and marriage from the stories my dad tells me, but I wanted to bring them up for a different reason, and this is because my grandma Springob demonstrated the definition of unconditional love for her husband when he was alive.

My grandpa, James Springob, was a great man, a man who served his country, loved his family, and was a devoted father to his kids. He died when I was ten years old, and I never got to know the James Springob everyone shares stories about from previous times. My grandpa suffered from Alzheimer's Disease, and it got worse as I grew old enough to remember him and develop a relationship with him. My memories of my grandpa unfortunately are my visits to him in the nursing home, a place that was terrifying for a kid to visit since the patients don't get to see children regularly. I don't remember ever having a conversation with my grandpa since he wasn't well, and it's made me sadder as I've gotten older to know I'll never get to know him like everyone else in my family did. It more recently though, has occurred to me how strong my grandma was in taking care of her husband through those rough years.

I don't ask about the details of my grandfather's

sickness very much, but my grandma told me one time about one of the first instances my grandpa had at a gas station. Grandma Springob was in the car waiting for Grandpa to fill the tank, but he was taking a while. So she got out and found him staring at what he was supposed to do.

"What's wrong Jim?" my grandma said.

"I…I don't remember how to fill the car with gas," my grandpa answered.

Grandma knew things were starting to get worse.

"Okay, you get back in the car," she said.

My grandma had never filled a car with gas until that day; it was something Grandpa always did. She had to ask a man for help because she didn't know what to do.

While I hate bringing this thought up, I could never imagine the pain of watching your spouse's memory and mind deteriorate like my grandpa's had from Alzheimer's, and along with that live through the day my grandma moved him into a nursing home, only to come home to a house that she now lived in alone. I absolutely detest mentioning this moment in my grandma's life, and I don't want this one moment that I discuss in their relationship to define my grandpa and grandma's marriage because I've heard so many fascinating and happy stories about their lives together. However, I want to remind people, of any age really, that *this* is what "for sickness and in health" and "till death do us part" mean. My grandma visited my grandpa *every single* day in the nursing home for what I believe to be almost ten years, and even after he passed, she continued to volunteer there. My grandma is a role model in the way she supported her husband during the worst part of his life. I know to my grandma it was second nature, but I also know not everyone could handle watching their spouse's memory fade away. My family believes my grandma Springob is in such great shape today due to the years she gave to taking care of her husband; it's either good karma or God's blessing upon her to live her life now that he's in peace.

When you're at the altar saying your vows, it's hard to imagine what could happen down the road with your spouse. But even though you don't know what's going to happen, you're saying you'll do whatever you can to support and love your person. I'm not sure either sets of grandparents ever thought they'd have so many years of happiness in their marriages, and I'm sure they didn't see the struggles until they were actually facing them. But they stuck it out, and that's what every old couple I've heard tells you; you've got to stick it out. Just because you're married doesn't mean you'll have a bad month or even year in your relationship. There's good times and bad times, but if you assume to always work it out rather than just call it quits, you'll get through it. Old people have a tendency to just tell it like it is, and they will be no different when giving you love advice, so listen to them...they know what they're talking about.

They won't be perfect.

Ladies, you know that list you have about what your dream guy needs to be? Well, like y'all I have one too; however, it has definitely become more negotiable.

We all have that person we will never get over, and Carson is that guy for me. I fell for him in seventh grade, always had it bad for him in high school, and will forever have a place for him in my heart. He really is the dream guy; he's cute, he has an absolutely fantastic family, he's religious, smart, caring, extremely giving, and he has eyes that still get me to this day. He set the standards I never realized I wanted in a guy until I met him. He was the person I waited for to enter the room, and when he left the room I felt there was no reason to be there anymore; and I still notice his presence when we're at the same event. From the big picture of Carson's life to his little quirks I never could get enough of any of it, and I still think nothing but the best of him. He honest to God changed my outlook on love and motivated me to find someone just as amazing. When I'm down about love, I think back to Carson, and I believe in magic all over again. He is the whole package. I've seen him be a fantastic boyfriend, and I know he'll be an incredible husband and father one day. Carson is the kind of guy who "checks everything off a girl's list."

And then there was Sean; the boy who I always had bad timing with. We always had that unspoken thing where we knew there was an attraction, but no one ever admitted it. Then he graduated and I forgot about it and put my attention back on Carson, though I knew that would never happen, either. It wasn't until Carson's graduation day that I caught up with Sean again. I saw him across from the bonfire at a graduation party that night. We caught up on everything in life, and eventually Sean and I exchanged numbers. I remember thinking *damn he looks good*. Sean was always one of the hot guys in high school, but college built him up even more in muscle and took away his Justin Bieber haircut (thank God!).

A couple days later I was working at the movie theatre when I got a text from Sean. We started texting more and more after that day, and before I knew it we both had told one another that we liked each other. When I finally had enough nerve, we went to a movie together. I hadn't had a guy pick me up and take me out in a *long* time, and I was sweating balls. I liked Sean, but I didn't feel the way I felt about Carson with him. Rather than feeling completely, absolutely sure like I had with Carson, I felt a bit doubtful. I liked Sean, but he wasn't everything *on my list*. But, he also was a lot of good things. The moment I got in the car for the movie Sean started playing a song.

"This is the song that reminds me of us," he said.

The song explained us perfectly.

We had a good time together; it was easy and fun. But we didn't hang out again like that until December, about five months later. We had been talking ever since then, but the next time we hung out was completely different. While it was a nice night to catch up, I was a nervous wreck. I had just endured a very stressful month, and the idea of a relationship was the last thing on my mind. I didn't feel sexy at that time in my life, rather just old and tarnished (yes I was eighteen; I know, I know, but senior year was taking the life out of me). We still had a good time catching up that December night, but I remember thinking *yea no, I'm not into him.* I hate saying that because it sounds so bitchy, but Sean is the person I could never decide yes or no with.

As usual, we continued to text about everyday. I may have had a tough time deciding whether I liked Sean enough to date him, but I will say this about him; he has been one of my biggest support systems in life since we've become close. My senior year of high school was a rough year. I had taken on realistically, too many leadership roles, and I was going nonstop for a straight nine months. When I look back at it now, I realize I wasn't in a good state of mind and I should've opened up more about it, but even though I didn't, Sean was my crutch. A simple text saying, "You'll be okay" was enough to get me through the rough days. He was always there to listen to me ramble, vent, or cry; and that meant everything. I didn't want someone giving me advice; I just wanted someone to listen.

I graduated high school in the nick of time before having a serious breakdown, and I had already told Sean that I officially decided I wanted to stay single. I never realized how much this hurt him until I came to UW-Stout in the fall. We started hanging out a lot, and once I finally felt I could be myself without a million hometown eyes on Sean and me, I realized I was ready to date him. I found a lot of comfort in Sean. I could hang out with him at midnight in sweatpants with no makeup on, and he didn't care! I even had my first college breakdown in front of him, and he didn't walk away. So when I told Sean that I was ready to date him and he said he couldn't because there was someone else he'd always liked in the picture, and thus he couldn't commit to me one hundred percent, I was crushed. I was more disappointed due to the fact that I had Sean to lean on for around a year and a half at that point, and now I had to go find someone else. But who would that someone else be?

I learned from Sean that there's something to be said for a guy who accepts you, flaws and all. The reason I decided I was ready to be Sean's girlfriend was because I weighed out the idea of perfect. Who did I *really* want; a boy like Carson who checks everything off my list, or someone like Sean who will listen to my problems and still think I'm sane at midnight when my mascara is running down my face in tears? Sean taught me that I don't want tall, dark, and handsome; I want a companion. Sean was not Carson by any means, but he also had characteristics that Carson didn't have. So I was willing to compromise. I was willing to listen to Sean's death metal music and cheer him on at his rugby games, because he was willing to support me in my crazy career dreams. I wanted to be his girl on the sidelines supporting him, because he was *always* there for me.

The summer after my freshman year of college, I was hanging out in my room one night after five straight days of work. I was exhausted, and suddenly I felt like something was missing in me. It was then that I realized I hadn't spoken or really seen Sean in almost a month, and the silence of the room reminded me how much I missed him. There's something really peculiar about silence; it's actually quite loud, and for most people silence needs to be filled with some type of stimulation, whether that's talking, turning on the T.V., or plugging in some headphones. People today don't know how to just *sit*, and they definitely don't know how to sit in silence with someone and welcome the lack of sound to the forefront. After finally catching a moment to breathe by myself on a quiet summer night, I started to cry, and I learned in that moment how important it is to find someone in life whom you can sit in pure silence without there being any awkwardness. I couldn't count the amount of times Sean and I would just chill after long days of classes, just watching a movie, saying *nothing* to each other, and yet everything was completely all right in the world. If we wanted to talk we did, but we didn't have to. We were comfortable around each other enough where we could be silent and okay with the quiet around us. That summer night I came to realize that I didn't necessarily lose out on that aspect of love by not dating Sean, but I needed that comfort of someone in my life again. And that comfort doesn't come from someone who "crosses everything off your list," it comes from someone who is your best friend. This idea of silence I'm sure sounds a little extravagant for people who haven't met their Sean in life, but once you do, you'll understand how much it means to be around someone who you don't constantly have to entertain but can still appreciate. And I think that's why we're all in this game of searching for love. We really are just trying to find our best friend.

A couple weeks after that summer night I was out east in Maryland for a family reunion, and we were at a family member's house that had a pet dog. I am deathly allergic to animals, to the point where I can walk into a house for five minutes and start to sneeze. I was discussing my allergies with a woman named Lisa, and turns out she has the same problems. She even went on to explain how her allergies affected her and her husband's stay on their honeymoon!

"We walked into the room of our hotel, and I could tell after about ten minutes that I was getting congested," Lisa told me, "and I felt bad, because I didn't want this issue to be a burden on our stay, and Richard had worked so hard to book the hotel, but he said, "I don't want you to feel sick this whole week, so if it's not going to work we can find another room." So we found a new room…and the same problem happened again! I thought *oh great this is such a wonderful start for him to be married to me,* but he was so calm about it and said, "Nope, let's find somewhere else." We finally found a new hotel where I didn't have any allergy problems, and we had a great time, but I was so grateful that he was understanding about it because unless people have allergies, it can be hard to grasp how much it affects your life."

"I know," I agreed, "and that's something I kind of always wonder about for when I move in with a guy because what if he has a dog or something and I'm allergic?"

"Exactly," Lisa said, "and you know, I don't know if you're dating anyone or anything, but you really do have to find someone who accepts those types of things about you. I was always nervous that I'd never find someone who would accept and understand my allergy issues, but Richard always has, and he's so caring about it all. It's funny, we were at dinner one night after we got married, and he turned to me and said, "I just kind of realized that I was always hoping and searching for my best friend, and after we got married I found that had been you all along." It even gives me goose bumps right now just thinking about it, but I agreed with him, and it's the best feeling to know you married your best friend."

That moment was one of those instances that I'll always cherish. I have so many weirdnesses that it'll be a miracle if I find someone who accepts them all. I deal with allergies everyday of my life, and when an attack comes on, my makeup is smeared off my face, my nose is red, and I can barely talk without snotting all over the place. I have and will always continue to have a bountiful amount of unattractive moments; I'm human. Therefore, while I previously stated that it's okay to say no to a nerd if you don't like them, I also say screw it to dating that *super* hot, supposedly popular guy. I'm the girl who tilts her head to the ground when I walk past a crazy good-looking guy. I don't feel qualified to talk to people on that level of pretty. I would be a nervous wreck around some perfect looking attractive boy, feeling like I'd have to impress them all the time. Give me a guy with brains or talent, a passion for what he's studying in school, or a good sense of humor. No one is going to be perfect, and let's be real; I know I'm sure as hell not perfect, either. I could and would never expect someone to "cross everything off my list" because I have plenty of flaws and probably also won't cross everything off my guy's list.

It's kind of humorous that I didn't get Carson, the guy who completed my list, or Sean, the guy who would've been a great companion, but I think I needed both Carson and Sean to teach me something important; your partner will not be perfect. They might like video games when you hate video games. They might be okay with staying in bed all Saturday while you have twenty projects to get finished. They might want a dog and you might not, or they might have a gluten allergy that affects what restaurant you can eat at. When you can recognize that your significant other is not going to be perfect, you will be able to see the details of creating your big picture–and realize it's way harder to officially create that. We don't think about the four years we have to spend studying at school, we just picture ourselves landing the dream job. The same goes for our relationships. We don't picture our person having an obsession with a weird eighties movie; we just see them being at least six feet tall and wanting children. But what about personality? What about maturity, the ability to comfort you when you're crying, the instinct of knowing when to say something or when to say nothing? I don't *really* know how Carson would've been in a situation had he been the one listening to me say in February 2012 how exhausted and angry I was constantly feeling. Sean wasn't perfect for me, and he definitely didn't cross everything off my list; but in our hey day, he was someone I fully trusted. I could tell him anything, and I knew he wouldn't judge; that's the kind of thing that should be number one on any person's list over height, career, or how many kids someone wants.

I believe that everyone needs a little bit of both Carson and Sean in a relationship in order for it to be successful. You should have some non-negotiable desires, but you shouldn't immediately count someone out because they aren't exactly what you were picturing. Who cares if they like baseball games and you like art museums; if you have the same morals, can you really go *that* wrong? I think it's good to learn how to love things you wouldn't regularly care about if those things are what make your person happy; it can make you get out of your comfort zone and try something different. However your values such as your religion, the time you spend with your parents, your desire to serve others; *those* types of ideals should never be compromised, they should be why your person loves *you*.

Before I met Sean, this was my list: Carson. After knowing both Carson and Sean, this is my list: someone who's fair, committed, faithful enough to at least give God a chance, someone who's tough, a hard worker, has a passion for life, makes the most of everyday and yet can teach me how to relax, and has eyes that make me melt. While it would be great for someone to be interested in things that I'm familiar with, I'm finding that people with different interests make me more motivated to become a part of their world. Everybody should have a base of key values they want their person to share, but we should also never forget to find that someone who loves us as much Saturday morning as they did Friday night.

*

So this big picture thing…it's kind of something that we need to have in order to set goals, but it's also something that will never end up looking how we imagine it. As we grow, our big picture will change in some ways. For some people maybe the big picture will be a totally different scene, and for others it may have minor changes in the details. But if you work hard in your relationships and in doing what you love, you can make your big picture your real life. You just have to remember to always be looking out for yourself. Never forget that love is respect, no matter if we're talking your friends, family, or significant others. You deserve to be around people who love you and bring you up, not down. If you're in a relationship that never makes you happy, or it leaves you constantly questioning what's going to happen next, move on. Relationships are meant to help you feel security, and if you don't have that it's not worth the hassle. When you do have something good though, trust your person when they're around people of the opposite sex; they're not going to cheat on you if they're into *you*. Make sure you understand the difference between what a marriage is compared to a wedding day, because not everyone does. As cheesy as it is, a good relationship takes teamwork, but that includes everyday teamwork and life teamwork; both are necessary. And though your person can be great, they won't be perfect; but that's okay. It's kind of part of the fun.

Reaching that moment when you can truly express who you are as an individual to the world is an award most people don't get, and to be able to bring that knowledge of who you are into your relationship is the grand prize. Maybe we don't always see it this way, but people are a huge component to the big picture. However, the big picture never really ends; it's something we're always going to aspire towards. Even when you think you've reached your big picture, you have to keep it updated, and that means you must continue to keep things in check with both others and yourself.

SO, WHAT IS YOUR
big picture?
WHAT WILL YOU THINK LOOKING BACK AT THE
little moments?

Drinking apple cider with caramel in a café in New York City. A home in Georgia, or a townhouse in Boston. Writing a T.V. show; writing anything, and something actually happening with it. A husband. Maybe one day a baby. That's my big picture.

A small town in Wisconsin. Sixty people I started kindergarten and graduated high school with. My family; visiting my family. Florida, Georgia. FFA. Feeling horrible and feeling wonderful. Feeling stuck; feeling like I know it all. Carson. Sean. Brad. Nerdy guys. Los Angeles. New York City. News reporting. Technology. Wanting something over there, but still being here. Still being single. Writing everything down. Listening. That's what I think of when I look back at my little moments.

And that's what I tell people about when I share my story.

I've accomplished a lot in a short amount of time, but I'll still be entering my quarter-life crisis single. It's not like I've never been close to being in a relationship. I've been attracted to a number of guys, I've gone on a couple dates (or should I say 'hang-outs' because it seems guys are scared of that other word), but I've never had a significant other. I've had luck in every other department of life besides romantic love.

Needless to say, being single my whole life has been frustrating. It affects my relationship with God. It's the reason that really makes me cry when five hundred other things have gone wrong. It never escapes my mind, especially when I see my friends happy with their significant others. I remember movie nights in high school becoming lame after I realized they were just cuddlefests. I was the pro at escaping the dance floor when the DJ played the slow tunes, and I have certainly seen my fair share of P.D.A. However, I have also watched a lot of relationships go sour. I've seen idiots break my friends' hearts, girls take their boyfriends for granted, people who can't be single for a second, and too many people who stress over really dumb things with their partner. I know people who have been married for over fifty years, people in long distance relationships, people who had a baby before marriage, and plenty of my friends are engaged or married already. Like I said before, I've seen a lot, but I haven't seen a lot of *me*– I haven't met very many people in a similar story like mine.

Being single has also taught me a lot about myself, and I'm extremely grateful for that. It has given me vast amounts of time to learn what I like, to practice my creativity, and put my goals into action. Though this is something that doesn't always have to do with love, I think it does in some ways, because a lot of people never give themselves time to discover who they are as one sole person walking this earth. To me, that is the most important thing. I would kill for cuddles and doing all those couple things that couples do, but I wouldn't trade knowing who I am as a person for anything.

I don't think love is all about finding "the one." I mean, it is about that, but "the one" is the big picture; it's Prince Charming or a sexy supermodel. I think love is really just about deciding the person you're with at that time is so great that you're ready to make them a part of your life…so you can enjoy the little moments together. Some people decide to do that at an early age, and some people wait until later on. Some people are relationship people and others are career people. All I know is if we all had the same story, things would be quite boring. So we shouldn't all want the same things; that's what makes the story interesting.

It makes sense now, when I look back at my story, why I'm still single; I've never been ready to make someone a significant part of my life. For most of my life, I've wanted five hundred things and hoped I could also balance a relationship along with it. But today it's different; if I can just have a location I love, doses of my favorite people to eat dinner with once in a while, and someone between all that to share the ups and downs with, I probably won't be happy all the time, and I'll probably still continue to reevaluate my story and where I'm at with my big picture, but I will love the little moments a lot.

I honestly don't believe you can have the best of both worlds with love and career success. We've seen too many people die with either a lot of money and no spouse, or die with little material items to give the world but someone next to their side. The people who succeed at love are people who are equal to each other in how much money they make or the amount of work and dedication they give to their jobs, be that a businessman or a homemaker. At some point, whether people are equal or not in comparison to all the crap they've accomplished, they both just have to get over themselves enough to respect one another. Eventually in a real relationship, the game changer one, the two people have to be willing to make sacrifices for one another. I hate writing that fact because that has been something I've been unwilling to do my entire life.

You are not your mother or father, no matter how good or bad they were to you. You are not your sibling or the cousin you get compared to at Christmas. You're not the housewife your boyfriend might want you to become, and you are not the douche bag your girlfriend dated in her last relationship. You are *you*. You don't have to be ready for marriage at age twenty-five like so many of your hometown friends were, you can go live

your life for a while and settle down later. You   are
allowed to go out and enjoy your life and do things the
way that will help *you* create *your* big picture. It's your
story, and everyone else around you is just a part of it. If
you go live a life that is just meant to impress people,
you're never going to reach your big picture, and the
moments you'll look back on will not make you happy. It
is okay to move to a new place, to feel sexy, to want
something different than what everyone around you
wants. You need to go find that thing, place, passion of
yours that makes you thrive, because that will lead you to
the success you're looking for, whether that's in a big
career or being a mommy or daddy. The reason you need
to find that success is so you don't feel like you need to
one-up your significant other when you find the right
person.

When two people have proved themselves equally to
the world in who they are and what they're skilled at, they
don't need to prove that to the person they're in a
relationship with. It's that unspoken thing that makes
you attracted to the other person. It's the spark when
you look at each other that shows you both just get it,
because you've been through the shitty moments in the
ways that were necessary for your individual self.

So with that, always be a keeper; what I mean by this
is be that person your significant other's friends and
family say, "Oh, he or she's a keeper." Be that good
person, always; it doesn't mean you're always happy, but
it means you're respectful and thoughtful of others, it
means you try.   Be the person in your story who really

made the effort to make their big picture a reality; because no matter where you end up, you won't regret the little moments when you look back.

Sometimes, what I've learned from never having a boyfriend really has nothing to do with the boyfriend part. But being single is part of my story. It's not part of my big picture, but it's definitely what I'll know contributed to making me happy when I look back at my little moments. I'm thankful that little moment of my friend complaining about her boyfriend while I was trying to eat my spinach salad happened, because it made me write a book and taught me how to embrace this singular situation. It helped me find my story. I am the same but different; like everyone else, all I want at the end of the day is love. The path I'm taking as a single lady is an unusual one, but my heart is telling me it is just as valuable and my brain has taken the action to share it. I'm the girl you'd expect to be just as busy dating as I am accomplishing my goals, but I'm not, and that's okay.

That's my story. What's yours?

"My wish is you, always."

FOLLOW
Stacey Springob

FACEBOOK.COM/SPRINSTA

TWITTER AND INSTAGRAM:
@STACEYSPRINGOB

HIRE
STACEY SPRINGOB
FOR YOUR NEXT
SPEAKING EVENT.

Contact

staceyspringob@hotmail.com